Fyodor Dostoevsky's
Crime and Punishment

A CASEBOOK

FYODOR DOSTOEVSKY'S
Crime and Punishment

◆ ◆ ◆

A CASEBOOK

Edited by
Richard Peace

OXFORD
UNIVERSITY PRESS

2006

OXFORD
UNIVERSITY PRESS

Oxford University Press, Inc., publishes works that further
Oxford University's objective of excellence
in research, scholarship, and education.

Oxford   New York
Auckland   Cape Town   Dar es Salaam   Hong Kong   Karachi
Kuala Lumpur   Madrid   Melbourne   Mexico City   Nairobi
New Delhi   Shanghai   Taipei   Toronto

With offices in
Argentina   Austria   Brazil   Chile   Czech Republic   France   Greece
Guatemala   Hungary   Italy   Japan   Poland   Portugal   Singapore
South Korea   Switzerland   Thailand   Turkey   Ukraine   Vietnam

Published by Oxford University Press, Inc.
198 Madison Avenue, New York, New York 10016

www.oup.com

Oxford is a registered trademark of Oxford University Press

Library of Congress Cataloging-in-Publication Data
Fyodor Dostoevsky's Crime and punishment: a casebook / edited by Richard Peace
p. cm—(Casebooks in criticism)
Includes bibliographical references and index.
ISBN-13 978-0-19-517562-2; 978-0-19-517563-9 (pbk.)
ISBN 0-19-517562-X; 0-19-517563-8 (pbk.)
1. Dostoyevsky, Fyodor, 1821–1881. Prestuplenie i nakazanie.   I. Title: Crime and punishment.
II. Peace, Richard Arthur.   III. Series.
PG3325.P73F965   2005
891.73'3—dc22   2005040654

1 3 5 7 9 8 6 4 2
Printed in the United States of America
on acid-free paper

Credits

◆　◆　◆

says on Dostoyevsky, edited by M. V. Jones and G. M. Terry, © Cambridge University Press, 1983. Reprinted by permission of Cambridge University Press.

Richard Peace, excerpt from *Dostoevsky: An Examination of the Major Novels*, published by Cambridge University Press, 1971. © 1992 Richard Peace.

V. E. Vetlovskaya, "Analiz epicheskogo proizvedeniya. Logika polozheniy v *Prestuplenii i nakazanii*," from *Dostoevsky: Materialy i issledovaniya*, No.14, Nauka, 1997, © 1997 V.E. Vetlovskaya. Printed with the permission of the author, and translated from the Russian by Richard Peace. Translation © Richard Peace, 2004

Edward Wasiolek, excerpt from *Dostoevsky: The Major Fiction*, The M.I.T. Press © 1964 by the Massachusetts Institute of Technology.

Acknowledgments

◆ ◆ ◆

I wish to thank Elissa Morris for her advice during my negotiations with publishers, also Valentina Vetlovskaya and Tatyana Kasatkina for their invaluable help with translation. I am indebted, too, to Dr. Jesse Edwards for technical aid provided.

Contents

◆　　◆　　◆

Note on Transliteration

◆　◆　◆

The transliteration of Russian into English is a notoriously chaotic affair. Those who attempt to adhere to a prescribed system inevitably come up against long-established usage at odds with their particular convention. This is particularly the case in literary criticism, where the choice of any given translation must inevitably impose its own conventions on the whole text. For the Introduction and the two articles translated from Russian I have relied on Jesse Coulson's translation of *Crime and Punishment* (Oxford University Press, World's Classics) and have, therefore, in these articles followed the system of transliteration which she herself adopted. Other contributions, relying on other translations, have been reprinted as they stand, and the reader will notice slight alterations in the spelling of names. Nevertheless the following variants should not cause confusion:

Dostoevsky/Dostoyevsky/Dostoevskii
Duklida/Duclida
Dunya/Dunia
Prestupleniye/Prestuplenie

Pulkheria/Pulkheriya/Pulcheria
Sonya/Sonia
Svidrigaylov/Svidrigailov
Vremya/Vremia
Zamëtov/Zamyotov/Zametov

Fyodor Dostoevsky's
Crime and Punishment

A C A S E B O O K

Introduction

❖   ❖   ❖

R EADING *CRIME AND PUNISHMENT* is a strong experience. It is the work of a writer whose whole life was
subject to strong experiences.

Dostoevsky was born in 1821 in a poor district of Moscow,
where his father was a doctor at a paupers' hospital. From an
early age he was aware of poverty, illness, and eccentricity. As the
second son of seven children brought up by an authoritarian
father, his upbringing was strict. At the age of sixteen he left for
the capital, St Petersburg, to study as a military engineer; Adele
Lindenmeyr will argue that Dostoevsky's own training as a
draughtsman and his study there of architectural history are reflected on the pages of *Crime and Punishment* in Raskolnikov's speculative plans for reshaping St Petersburg. Eighteen months into
his course he learned of the death of his father, who was rumored
to have been murdered by his own peasants. Later scholarship
questions this assumption, as it does Freud's assertion that news
of his father's death led to Dostoevsky's first epileptic fit. Nevertheless, the small inheritance he received enabled Dostoevsky in

1844 to apply for release from his military service in order to devote himself to a literary career.

After a modest start, translating Balzac's *Eugénie Grandet*, his very first original work brought him dizzying success. He was acclaimed a genius, literally overnight, on the strength of the manuscript of his short novel *Poor Folk* (published 1846). The eminent literary critic Belinsky rapturously welcomed it as a major contribution to a literary trend he himself was at pains to establish—the so-called Natural School, with its emphasis on the depiction of the lower reaches of urban life and the fate of the "little man."

However, this sudden elevation to the status of genius presented difficulties for Dostoevsky's highly-strung temperament. His behavior alienated other writers such as Turgenev and even Belinsky himself, who found Dostoevsky's subsequent works, for all their urban setting, difficult to accommodate within the parameters of the Natural School. Nevertheless, the very concept which lay behind *The Double* (1846) and the depiction of dream states and delirium in *The Landlady* (1847) not only anticipate crucial aspects of *Crime and Punishment*, but are typical of Dostoevsky's later writing as a whole. More specifically, Wasiolek sees Golyadkin, the hero of *The Double*, as in some sense anticipating Raskolnikov.

Sentimentalism is a further element in Dostoevsky's early depiction of the urban theme; it is present in *Poor Folk* and quite pronounced in such works as *A Faint Heart* (1848) and *White Nights* of the same year, with its subtitle "A Sentimental Novel." In *Crime and Punishment* the sentimental theme may be detected in Dostoevsky's treatment of the various members of the Marmeladov family—a subplot that Wasiolek considers "almost a paradigm of the sentimental situation."

The year 1848 was, in fact, a turning point in European history. It was the year of revolutions throughout the continent, and in Russia a jittery regime paid particular attention to any signs of local dissidence. Dostoevsky had already moved away from the orbit of Belinsky towards a more politically motivated group—the Petrashevsky circle.

In the early hours of a May morning in 1845 two fellow writers, who had spent the night reading the manuscript of *Poor Folk*, had descended on him to proclaim him a genius. Four years later, at a similar hour in April of 1849, the police burst in on his flat to arrest him as a criminal. The Manichean polarity of these two events not only affected the course of his life, but would also leave their dialectic signature on his writing. He and his fellow "conspirators" were whisked away to the Peter and Paul Fortress, where they were kept under interrogation well into December. In *Crime and Punishment* Porfiry's sophisticated methods of criminal investigation may well owe a debt to the author's own experience, yet, unlike Raskolnikov, he appears to have outwitted his interrogators by managing to hide the fact of his deeper involvement in would-be political activity than the mere public reading of a subversive letter—the charge finally brought against him. Nevertheless, for this he was condemned to death by firing squad.

In reality this sentence was to be a terrifying charade. In spite of the fact that everything was carried out with exactitude—rifles, blindfolds, drums, a priest, even coffins, the czar intended to pardon them. At the very last moment a messenger arrived; the death sentence was commuted to penal servitude in Siberia, followed by exile there. Facing up to the imminence of death was undoubtedly one of the "strongest" experiences undergone by Dostoevsky—it is a theme he returns to more than once in his writing, and, as Valentina Vetlovskaya points out, faced with the inevitability of committing the crime, Raskolnikov himself feels like a man condemned to death. Later he muses on the determination of a man so condemned to cling on to life even if it were "on a ledge so small that there was no more than room for his two feet" [152].[1]

In all, Dostoevsky spent four years in the penal settlement at Omsk alongside murderers and other criminals. He gives a fictional account of this experience in *Notes from the House of the Dead* (1860–61). His association, even identification, with some of its worst inmates gave him a privileged insight into the criminal mind. Moreover, the more sympathetic attitude of Orthodox Christianity to the criminal, with its exhortation to charity and the giving of alms—reflected in the view of the common people that convicts were merely "unfortunate ones" (*neschastnye*)—also contributed to the author's less condemnatory attitude towards his criminal hero in *Crime and Punishment*, cemented by his new-found religious faith. The antirationalistic nature of such faith is epitomised in a letter he wrote on leaving the Omsk penal settlement: "If someone proved to me that Christ was other than the truth, and it *really* might be that the truth was other than Christ, then I would rather remain with Christ than with the truth."[2] A similar nonrationalist, Christian approach is reflected in the final two chapters of the Casebook, the first of which examines the novel in terms of the "other world," the second through the significance of its iconography.

Dostoevsky began his Siberian exile in 1854, and in 1857 married Mariya Isaeva, the widow of a local minor civil servant. On his honeymoon he suffered a severe fit, and later in the year epilepsy was diagnosed, the onset of the disease being officially recorded as 1850. His marriage seemed doomed from the start. A consumptive and querulous wife and a serious, disabling disease were further "strong experiences" to add to his burdens, yet both would find expression in his writing. The cantankerous behavior of Katerina Ivanovna, the consumptive widow of the minor civil servant Marmeladov in *Crime and Punishment*, may owe something to Mariya and her drunken first husband, Isaev. Epilepsy, too, would become a theme in later novels.

Despite a change of regime in 1855, and the wish of the new czar, Alexander II, to introduce more liberal policies, Dostoevsky was not allowed back to St Petersburg until 1860, and, even upon his return, was long kept under police surveillance. The Russia of the 1860s was a country in social and intellectual ferment. The younger generation of thinkers, led by Chernyshevsky, Dobrolyubov, and the even more radical Pisarev, were loosely branded "nihilists," as though in the mould of the hero of Turgenev's novel *Fathers and Children*. In fact they were, for the most part, adherents of the doctrine of "enlightened self-interest" propounded by the English Utilitarian thinkers J. Bentham and J. S. Mill, but in its more radical Russian reformulation as "rational egoism." Their view of man was simple; his religious nature, expressed in the *dualism* of body and soul, was rejected in favor of *monism*—all psychological and spiritual phenomena were merely an expression of man's physical being.

In 1864 Dostoevsky launched an attack on such ideas in his *Notes from Underground*, which may be seen as his own "nihilistic" demolition of "nihilism," but the polemic also surfaces on the pages of *Crime and Punishment*, principally in the extravagant ideas of Lebezyatnikov and Luzhin. At the same time the intellectual ferment of the 1860s influenced *Crime and Punishment* in a much more fundamental way—Raskolnikov himself is caught up by the swirl of extreme ideas. In *Notes from Underground* Dostoevsky had also wished to put forward positive, religious ideas, but they were suppressed by the censor (much as later such ideas had to be toned down in *Crime and Punishment*). *Notes from Underground* is often seen as a precursor of existentialism. In particular the concept of the "wall"—a symbol of a barrier that may not be crossed—seems also to have relevance for Raskolnikov's crime. His striving to cross the wall and "choose himself" in itself betrays an existentialist element.

Before *Notes from Underground*, however, although times had changed, Dostoevsky was still trying his hand at the old style of writing: the depiction of oppressed people in the environment of the city and surrounded by an atmosphere of sentiment. Nevertheless, his short novel *The Insulted and the Injured* (1861) also contained some new elements—a Svidrigaylov-like villain in Prince Valkovsky and the appearance of a detective. In fact, he had made an impressive comeback on the literary scene as the acclaimed author of *The House of the Dead*, and co-editor with his brother Mikhail of two journals, *Time* [*Vremya*] (1861–63) and *Epoch* [*Epokha*] (1864–65). However, further trials awaited him. *Time* was closed down by the government, and the new journal *Epoch* struggled to survive financially. His wife, Mariya, died in April 1864, followed by the even greater blow in July of the death of his beloved brother Mikhail. Dostoevsky was desperately in debt, but he added further to his woes by seeking another "strong experience": he indulged a manic passion for gambling.

In the ledgers of the now closed-down *Epoch,* Dostoevsky adumbrated a story about the evils of drink—a theme later incorporated in the plot-line of the Marmeladov family—but it was in Wiesbaden in the late summer of 1865, having lost all his money at the casino and shut up in his hotel room, unable to pay his bill or afford proper meals, that Dostoevsky conceived the idea of *Crime and Punishment*. The dreamer isolating himself from human contact, starving in his cheap room, and desperately planning through a "murder" to extricate himself from his dire position—in all this Dostoevsky seems psychologically close to his own hero. He offered his novel to the publisher Katkov in a letter, which clearly outlines his original intentions. It was to be about a crime related to "ideas that were in the air."

Yet the acceptance of his novel did not fully save him. He had already concluded a contract with a rogue publisher Stellovsky to bring out an edition of his collected works up to that date, plus a new novel. If this new work were not delivered by a deadline, he would lose the copyright on his writing for nine years, yet at the same time he was also working on *Crime and Punishment* for Katkov. His recent "strong experiences," yet again, provided him with a theme: the novel for Stellovsky would be entitled *The Gambler*, but to finish it on time he had to fall back on the services of a stenographer, Anna Snitkina. With her help he not only fulfilled his publisher's contract, but in turn offered her a marital one. She accepted, and not only saved Dostoevsky from Stellovsky, but also took down the concluding sections of *Crime and Punishment*. Like Raskolnikov at the novel's end, Dostoevsky may also be said to have found his Sonya. Indeed, Anna through many tribulations was to prove a firm rock of stability and his salvation.

It is obvious that the genesis of *Crime and Punishment* is the interweaving of many strands, the unraveling and explication of which is a chief objective for the present study. In simple terms, however, the plot focuses relentlessly on Raskolnikov, a drop-out student, who chooses to live half-starving in a tiny, rented room in St Petersburg, refusing all help, even from his friend Razumikhin. We learn that he is planning to murder an old-woman money-lender, Alëna, and profit from her wealth, whether for ideological or personal motives is never quite clear. The backdrop for the drama is the poverty of the mean streets of St Petersburg and its underclass; in an early foray into the city, he meets the drunkard Marmeladov and learns of his daughter, Sonya—a prostitute full of Christian virtue. When he kills Alëna he is also forced to kill her half-sister, Liza, who inopportunely comes in on the scene of the crime. After the bungled murder Raskolnikov falls into a feverish state and often behaves as though he wishes to betray himself, so that the detective Porfiry begins to suspect him purely on psychological grounds. A chaste relationship develops between Raskolnikov and Sonya (who has links with the murdered Liza) and Raskolnikov confesses his crime to her. The confession is overheard by Svidrigaylov, a shadowy figure associated with vile deeds, whose aim is to seduce Raskolnikov's sister, Dunya. Svidrigaylov appears to have a hold over Raskolnikov, but when he unexpectedly commits suicide, Raskolnikov goes to the police himself to confess. He is condemned to penal servitude in Siberia. Sonya follows him, and the Epilogue holds out hope for Raskolnikov's moral regeneration under her influence.

Dostoevsky, as we have seen, began by translating Balzac, then pursued his own literary career through the theme of the city, prominent in writers of the Natural School of the 1840s. Donald Fanger in his essay "Apogee: *Crime and Punishment*" (chapter 1) sheds light on both these literary influences on the novel, in particular Dostoevsky's relationship to Balzac and French literature, as well as to later developments in Russian writing on the theme of the city. There are two distinct trends in the depiction of St Petersburg: the "romantic" and the "realistic," to borrow Fanger's terminology. Before the so-called Natural School, both Pushkin and Gogol had portrayed St Petersburg as a fantastic city, whose very nature conditioned unusual events. It is this aspect which some of Dostoevsky's early stories (*The Double* and *The Landlady*) reflect, and, indeed, in *Notes from Underground* its hero considers St Petersburg to be "the most abstract and premeditated town in the whole of the world." On the other hand, those writers who sought to develop the physiological sketch of the Natural School on into the 1860s strove to achieve greater realism. Two, in particular, were closely acquainted with Dostoevsky and contributed to his journal *Time*: Vsevolod Krestovsky (mentioned by Fanger) and N. G. Pomyalovsky (referred to in my essay, "Motive and Symbol," chapter 4).[3]

Krestovsky's mammoth novel *The Slums of St Petersburg* (a section of which was published in 1864 in Dostoevsky's second journal *Epoch*) is set in the very same area of St Petersburg as *Crime and Punishment*. The section published in *Epoch* depicted a low tavern nicknamed the "Ruffs" (*Ershi*), which Krestovsky suggests is entirely typical. Superficially it looks forward to the tavern that Raskolnikov enters at the end of the first chapter of *Crime and Punishment*, but for all the similarities of ambience, the differences are quite striking. In Dostoevsky such squalor serves as a background for the mock sentimental confession of Marmeladov. Krestovsky's tavern is quite clearly presented as a den of thieves, where customers such as Marmeladov could easily be stripped of all they stand up in. In fact, the Haymarket district of Krestovsky's realistic novel bristles with thieves, cutthroats, and horribly ruthless beggars. It allows us to see just how selective Dostoevsky has been in his use of realistic detail. His streets and drinking dens do not teem with murderers and thieves, who might shade out and distract from the ideologically inspired crime of Raskolnikov. The one "criminal" to act as a "foil" is his intellectual double, Svidrigaylov. Dostoevsky gives us no real beggars. The nearest he comes to this is the portrayal, typical of the Natural School, of the street musician, but here the emphasis is on the mood the scene inspires in Raskolnikov: its significance is aesthetic rather than ethical. Raskolnikov himself is given alms at one point as though he were a beggar, but Katerina Ivanovna begging on the street with her children stands out starkly, almost as a unique event. If, by isolating such events from the actual reality of the streets, Dostoevsky is seeking to give clarity to their particular significance and pathos, his approach seems almost the opposite when it comes to his treatment of prostitution. The position of Sonya is bolstered, and given tacit support, by the lot of young women on the streets of the capital: the young woman pursued by a roué; the seamstress who tries to drown herself; the young prostitute Duklida; even his own sister, pursued by Svidrigaylov.

Their fate elicits from Raskolnikov a short disquisition on society's attitude to prostitution, and these figures provide a social context for understanding the plight of Sonya herself. The street scene with the organ-grinder and Duklida occurs in part 2, chapter 6; its detail, Fanger says, "makes it the physiological sketch par excellence." He is right—it looks back to the Natural School of the 1840s rather than reflecting Krestovsky's account of a more crime-ridden St Petersburg.

Interestingly enough, Krestovsky's novel also depicts the attempted murder and plundering of a moneylender, but it is an act of sheer criminality, which in the end is frustrated. To see intellectual justification for crime one has to turn to Pomyalovsky, in particular his unfinished novel *Brother and Sister* (Krestovsky was accused, though probably unjustly, of having plagiarized the manuscript for his own novel). Of these two contemporary writers, Dostoevsky is intellectually nearer to Pomyalovsky, though the novel of Krestovsky undoubtedly casts a different light on the "realism" of the cityscape in *Crime and Punishment*.

Fanger refers to the Napoleonic motif in the novel, which is associated as much with Napoleon III as with his uncle. Adele Lindenmeyer links this to the theme of St Petersburg, and here Raskolnikov's Napoleonic aspirations are seen in a more constructive context; he not only has a vision of the "New Jerusalem," but of a new reordered St Petersburg, fit for its ordinary citizens to live in—a city redesigned along the lines of a Paris reconstructed by Napoleon III and his prefect Haussman.

Edward Wasiolek sees many strands of Dostoevsky's earlier writing reflected in *Crime and Punishment*, but points to the sudden emergence of crime as a central theme in the novel and later works. In a stimulating argument he shows us that, after committing his murders, Raskolnikov "is not running *away* from the crime but *toward* it." The novels of Dostoevsky have often been criticized for their prolixity and apparent lack of discipline. My own chapter on motif and symbol in *Crime and Punishment* seeks to emphasize structure in the novel, pointing to patterns, recurrent themes, and psychological motives linked to the overall symbolic framework of the work.

The writings of Dostoevsky have long attracted the attention of professional psychologists—most famously Freud. If some aspects of Dostoevsky's work seem to anticipate Freudian theory (for instance the role of the unconscious, which, in part 6, chapter 3 of the novel, Svidrigaylov seems to suggests lies behind Raskolnikov's "chance" meeting with him in a restaurant), it must be borne in mind that Freud himself came out of an already existing tradition, and that Dostoevsky was aware of the writings of such earlier psychologists as C. G. Carus.[4] In two separate sections of *Self and Others* the professional psychologist R. D. Laing gives a detailed analysis of what he sees as key episodes in the novel: Raskolnikov's dream of the beating of the old mare; and the reading of the letter from his mother. He reproduces these quotations at length in order to convey their full psychological impact on hero and reader alike.

In his letter offering the novel to Katkov Dostoevsky had linked Raskolnikov's crime to "ideas that are in the air," and it may come as a surprise to learn that such extreme notions had an English source. Raskolnikov's biological explanation for the emergence of a "genius" out of the mass of common humanity has strong Darwinian overtones, but it is English utilitarian thought that is most clearly referred to. As early as chapter 2 of the novel Marmeladov quotes Lebezyatnikov "who is a follower of the latest ideas" to the effect that compassion is actually prohibited by science: "That is how they order things in England, where they have political economy" [11–12]. The reference is to the laissez-faire economic ideas of Jeremy Bentham and John Stuart Mill, with their utilitarian doctrine of "enlightened self-interest" (though now inverted, by a Russian mirror with a distorting focus, into a socialist doctrine). The "scientific" justification for disregarding compassion is obviously related to Raskolnikov's crime, and the link is made even more specifically in the modern "economic" arguments of Luzhin, who justifies his own grasping self-interest by reference to such fashionable ideas. The doctrine of "love yourself," he says, has replaced the older precept of "love your neighbour" [142], to which Raskolnikov himself later counters that, if these ideas were taken to their logical conclusion, it would mean that you could cut people's throats [145]. In essence, of course, the polemic is a Russian one, and Dostoevsky has in his sights the home-grown followers of utilitarian thought, Chernyshevsky, Dobrolyubov and Pisarev. The nature of this Russian polemic is examined by Derek Offord in the context of the causes of crime and the meaning of law.

When Dostoevsky came back from his ten-year "deep freeze" in Siberia the sudden confrontation with the intellectual climate of the 1860s, compared with the Russia he had left in the more romantically and aesthetically inclined atmosphere of the 1840s must have been a considerable shock. Chernyshevsky's novel *What Is To Be Done?* (1864) was rapidly seen as a textbook for the younger generation, instructing them how to conduct themselves: its principal doctrine was "rational egoism." Polemicizing with this in *Crime and Punishment*, Dostoevsky, as we have seen, cleverly returns Chernyshevsky's doctrine back to its English roots, and in the figure of Luzhin reveals it as a bourgeois justification for rank self-interest, and essentially anti-Christian in nature.

A more extreme doctrine of egoism could be seen in the writings of D. I. Pisarev, who was a growing force in the mid-1860s. He is principally remembered for his championship of Turgenev's "nihilistic" hero Bazarov and for his essay "The Destruction of Aesthetics," which made him the chief ideologue of the fashion to denounce aesthetic criteria, that so gripped the younger generation of the 1860s. Anti-aestheticism is an important element in Raskolnikov's perception of his crime. He tries purposely to live as squalidly as possible, and finds solace in the cheerless music of a street musician amid drab surroundings, yet is strangely, and unaccountably, disturbed by the beauty of another view of St Petersburg, with the river, the palace and the marvelous dome of the cathedral [108]. Unlike the illustrious "crimes" of Napoleon, he chooses the most unaesthetic of bloody deeds to prove himself—the murder of a defenseless old woman:

Napoleon, the pyramids, Waterloo—and a vile, withered old woman, a moneylender, with a red box under her bed— what a mishmash even for someone like Porfiry Petrovich to digest! . . . How could he, indeed? Aesthetic considerations forbid. "Does Napoleon crawl under an old woman's bed?" he will say. Oh, what rubbish! . . . [263]

Later in an effort to justify himself to his sister Dunya, he attempts to shift the ground of his defeat from ethics to aesthetics: "Ah, it's the form that's wrong, the form is not aesthetically satisfactory!" [499].

The figure of Napoleon lurks behind Raskolnikov's division of humanity into "heroes" and "the crowd," but as Fanger and many other commentators have pointed out the chief influence here is *The History of Julius Caesar*, a work by Napoleon III, in which he sought to justify the actions of his uncle. At the same time, as we have seen, there is clearly a Darwinian element present in Raskolnikov's speculation on the processes of selection, and the more extreme, almost aristocratic, perception of egoism that lay behind Pisarev's promotion of the "thinking realist" is also an influence.

The final two chapters of the Casebook are devoted to another important strand in Dostoevsky's novel—its religious significance. Much has already been written on this in the West, but after the fall of the Soviet Union it became a topic which Russian scholars themselves could address. They came to it afresh, bringing to bear their own inner knowledge of the Orthodox mind and its spiritual traditions.

If Offord looks at crime from a philosophical and legal standpoint, Vetlovskaya puts it in a religious context. In Russian literary criticism, as in Orthodox theology, there is a tradition of textual exegesis focusing on diabolic forces. Vetlovskaya pursues an argument based on references to the devil and the "other world," some of which are not always explicit for the non-Russian reader and require further elucidation in the notes. At the same time her article leavens Orthodox theology with more modern literary technique—linguistic analysis.

Whereas Vetlovskaya's approach to the Christian theme of the novel is linguistic, that of Kasatkina is more visual and iconographic. One of the problems facing all commentators on the novel is its ending, which deals with Raskolnikov's love for Sonya in the penal settlement and the promise of his moral resurrection. Wasiolek believes it would have been better to have ended the novel with Raskolnikov's confession, and to many critics the writing in the Epilogue appears thin, the narrative sketchy and the promise held out for Raskolnikov's redemption unconvincing. Kasatkina tackles the issue head on, relying less on the purely literary values of the text than on what she sees as its iconographic suggestiveness. At the same time she adapts more recent western literary theory to her method; for just as a "reading" may be created through the interaction of author, reader and text, so, too, a visual "reading" may be achieved through a similar interaction—the "creation" of an icon.

The hero's name, in itself, has religious overtones: the word *raskol* means "schism," but there is a certain ambiguity here. Earlier, in an article of 1864, Dostoevsky had noted a schism among the nihilists—the followers of Chernyshevsky versus those of Pisarev.[5] Nevertheless, the name itself is derived from *raskol'nik*—a religious schismatic, and the suggestion that Raskolnikov is in some sense a religious rebel, an "unorthodox" apostate, is reinforced by further symbolism in the novel. Moreover, it is an interesting fact that in Dostoevsky's later novels his murderers are all linked in some sense to sectarianism.

The many strands that interweave throughout the novel produce a complicated but rich texture. It is a highly original work. The fact that Raskolnikov totally dominates the pages of the novel and forces his reader into a perhaps unwished for empathy—recoiling when Raskolnikov appears about to be caught or betray himself; breathing relief when the danger is past—these are reactions which identify the reader totally with the murderer, and not just any murderer, but one who commits a particularly vile and bloody crime. In literature such direct empathy with the criminal had not been attempted before Dostoevsky. One may cite Macbeth and perhaps other Shakespearian villain/heroes, but for all their soliloquies, they are still figures out there on stage; they are not in the reader's own mind and there in the room. The space Raskolnikov inhabits is the reader's own personal one.

There had been criminal heroes before in folklore and popular literature, but Raskolnikov is not the romanticized "do-gooder" Robin Hood nor the ruthless rebel Pugachev of Russian folklore and literature; in his claim for his reader's total empathy he is a completely new criminal "hero." One can see the roots of this empathy in the Orthodox feeling of compassion towards the criminal, the "unfortunate one," also in Dostoevsky's own enforced self-identification with such people in the penal settlement, but Dostoevsky has gone beyond this and opened up subconscious wells of darkness within his readers themselves. The novel was a shock to the bourgeois smugness of much of nineteenth-century morality. Yet, in the next century many followed where Dostoevsky had led, so that one may say that now there has actually developed a cult of the criminal as hero, not merely in literature, but in art, television and cinema. Dostoevsky's "strong experiences" have left a powerful legacy.

Notes

1. The numbers in square brackets are references to pages in: Fyodor Dostoevsky, *Crime and Punishment*, translated by Jesse Coulson, with an introduction and notes by Richard Peace, New York, Oxford University Press, 1995. It is this edition which will be referred to in the Introduction and the two final chapters translated from Russian (though there may be some minor revisions to accommodate linguistic interpretations in the latter two cases). Elsewhere the various sources of translation used in the original articles have been preserved.

2. See F. M. Dostoevsky, *Polnoe sobranie sochinenii v tridtsati tomakh*, Leningrad, 1972–1990, vol. 28(1), p.176. Hereafter referred to as *PSS*, followed by volume number and page.

3. See also Richard Peace, *Dostoyevsky: An Examination of the Major Novels*, Cambridge, Cambridge University Press, 1971, pp.27–28.

4. See Maria Kravchenko, *Dostoevsky and the Psychologists*, Amsterdam, Verlag Adolf M. Hakkert, 1978, p.157

5. "Gospodin Shchedrin, ili raskol v nigilistakh," *PSS*, Vol. 20, pp.102–120.

Apogee: *Crime and Punishment*

DONALD FANGER

◆   ◆   ◆

> Dismal, foul, and stinking summertime Petersburg
> suits my mood and might even give me some false
> inspiration for the novel.
> —DOSTOEVSKY, letter of 1865

CRIME AND PUNISHMENT IS THE FIRST—and arguably the greatest—product of that special realism toward which Dostoevsky had been groping for twenty years; it is unquestionably his greatest Petersburg work. *The Insulted and Injured* had given him the secret of uniting several plots into a single entity, and *Notes from Underground* the secret of transmuting his new ideological concerns into the stuff of fiction. The result, like *Hamlet,* is a metaphysical thriller, a point that critics writing in English cannot be accused of neglecting. What they have tended to neglect is the fact that this is also the first great Russian novel to deal with the life of the one city in Russia that could be compared to the capital cities of the West. A brief historical excursus will show how this is so.

The novel was originally conceived in terms that suggest Zola. Projected under the title of "The Drunkards," it was to deal "with the present question of drunkenness . . . [in] all its ramifications, especially the picture of a family and the bringing up of children in these circumstances, etc., etc."[1] Once Dostoevsky conceived

Raskolnikov and his crime, of course, this theme became auxiliary, centering on the story of the Marmeladov family. But even apart from them, it runs like a red thread through the novel. Marmeladov is the first and most important, but hardly the last, of the drunkards Raskolnikov meets, and he himself is taken for one more than once. The sympathetic Razumikhin meets his friend's mother and sister in a state of intoxication; Porfiry pointedly remarks that he does not drink; Raskolnikov's fateful interviews with Zametov and Svidrigailov take place in taverns. The reason for the prevalence of this motif is not far to seek: it was, like so much else in the novel, a particularly acute social problem of the day. In 1860 the government had projected a new system of excise taxes, hoping to control the consumption of alcohol more effectively. Its hopes proved illusory, but they were shared at the time by Dostoevsky's own journal, *Vremya* (Time), which in 1861 devoted a long article to drunkenness in France and particularly to the family side of the question. Again in 1865, when Dostoevsky was beginning work on the novel, the government set up a commission to review the whole question of the "excessive use" of alcohol among the people, provoking a whole series of journalistic comments. As Leonid Grossman has noted, "against the background of these numerous articles disclosing the connection of alcoholism with prostitution, tuberculosis, unemployment, destitution, abandoned children, and the physical dying-out of whole families, the main lines of the story of the Marmeladovs emerge with full clarity."[2] Grossman goes on to say that, in contrast to the Falstaffian tradition of treating this theme in literature, Dostoevsky introduces for perhaps the first time its tragic side; in this, he parallels the innovation of his revered Pushkin, who similarly reversed a comic tradition in his "Covetous Knight," where he turned a tragic light on the figure of the miser (some three years before the appearance of Balzac's Grandet).

The theme of prostitution is closely connected with that of drunkenness, not only in the figure of Sonya but in a number of incidental figures—the seduced girl whom Raskolnikov rescues from her lecherous pursuer, the girl who attempts suicide in the canal, the procuress Louisa Ivanovna, the attractive Duclida. Here, too, he was exploiting an issue of immediate public concern. His own journal had printed in 1862 an article by one M. Rodevich entitled "Our Social Morality," which bespoke sympathy for "fallen women," tracing hunger and poverty as among the chief causes of prostitution and noting, "not infrequently even a mother will sell her daughter into vice because of oppressive poverty."[3] The writer argues that one cannot condemn these daughters "of civil servants who are retired or have large families, or of rich men who have squandered their money": these are women "who have nothing to eat, who are consumed by need, pricked by the needle which provides a pitiful maintenance of pennies for laborious work."[4] One recalls Marmeladov's pathetic account of Sonya's efforts to live as a seamstress. Equally striking in its pertinence to the novel is the point of another article in the same journal, entitled "Remarks on the Question of Social Morality" and signed only "P. S." Here the author goes beyond the question of sympathy for the prostitute. "The external manifestations of vice," he finds, "differ essentially from the internal, and one cannot combine them in one unbroken link. One can meet in a single evening a hundred prostitutes on any fine, brightly lighted street, and nevertheless have not the slightest notion of the state of their morality. To get this notion, it would be necessary to be transported into their internal world, and look at their behavior from there, from the new standpoint." The author sees this as a major literary problem and calls upon contemporary writers to produce "five or six stories of the life of prostitutes, honestly told with all the details and with psychological indications."[5] Dostoevsky, whether deliberately or not, did answer this call: after Liza in *Notes from Underground* came Sonya; and after her the kept women, Nastasya Filippovna and Grushenka.

As it was with alcoholism and prostitution, so with the theme of crime. In the story of Raskolnikov, a number of impulses from the concerns of the day converge. There is, first of all, the fact that at this time Russian juridical thought, and especially criminology, was undergoing a renewal. Grossman thinks it likely that Dostoevsky himself was responsible for the editorial commentaries on a host of articles in his journals dealing with murder, robbery, and the efficacy of legal punishment. Besides theoretical pieces, moreover, he printed a long series entitled, "From the Criminal Affairs of France," which he commended as being "more engrossing than any possible novels because they [the trial accounts] illuminate such dark sides of the human soul, which art is not fond of touching on—so that if it does touch on them, it does so only in passing, in the form of episodes."[6] Included in the series was the case of Lacenaire, whom Dostoevsky characterized in an editorial note as "a phenomenal, enigmatic, fearful, and interesting figure."[7] What is more striking is a whole set of parallels between Lacenaire, as described in *Vremya,* and Raskolnikov. The young Frenchman is pictured as having features that were "fine and not without nobility. On his ironical lip there trembled constantly a ready sarcasm." He wanted to devote himself to the study of law and afterwards referred to himself, falsely, as a "student of law." Jailed in 1829 for killing Benjamin Constant's nephew in a duel, he dabbled in literature and on his release, along with a former fellow prisoner, used a three-edged rasp to kill one Chardon and his elderly mother. After the robbery—like Raskolnikov—he found two visitors asking for Chardon at the unlocked door, and with minor differences of detail he avoided being recognized in much the same way.[8]

Finally, one more topical item, closer to home, may have contributed to the writing of *Crime and Punishment.* In the spring of 1865, just when Dostoevsky was forming the idea of his novel, the Petersburg newspapers were filled with detailed stenographic accounts of the trial of Gerasim Chistov, who had killed two old women with a short-handled ax and robbed them of over eleven thousand rubles.[9]

The very theme of money, moreover, struck so forcibly at the beginning and throughout the novel, was of particular pertinence just at this moment. It is true, of course, that Dostoevsky had always made the effects of money, or its absence, a key factor in his fiction, as the title of his first work indicates. But money plays a different role here—a role related as much to the world of *Le Père Goriot* as to that of *Poor Folk.* For the first time the figure of the predator becomes important (Alyona Ivanovna, Luzhin), and the temptation to quick riches immediate and compelling. As Paris and London had done some decades before, Petersburg was becoming a capitalist city, like them subject to new and severe financial crises. One such crisis was acute in the early sixties, and Dostoevsky's *Vremya,* along with the rest of the press, was full of articles about it; one of 1863 was entitled "Where Has Our Money Gone?" and discussed "the commercial, industrial, and financial crisis hanging over us."[10] The situation reached its peak in 1865, the year Dostoevsky began *Crime and Punishment.* He felt the pinch himself, for he had to liquidate his publishing business, making for catastrophic losses in subscriptions. As Grossman sums it up: "Journals were closing down, general credit was falling improbably, the government was issuing loan after loan, the money market was overflowing with paper tokens, the government exchequer was 'oppressed' with a deficit. Such was the year when compassionate passers-by held out a penny on the street to the student Raskolnikov, and the titular councillor Marmeladov created his variation on the folk saying: " 'Poverty is not a vice, but destitution, sir, destitution is a vice, sir.' "[11]

Balzac had referred repeatedly to Rastignac as "one of those young men who . . ."—and Dostoevsky evidently intended Raskolnikov also to represent a trend. He was one of the "new men." Half a year before Dostoevsky began work on *Crime and Punishment,* his journal, *Epokha,* printed an article by Strakhov which claimed as the most striking feature of the time the fact that "Russian literature is troubled by the thought of the new men."[12] Turgenev's Bazarov had been the first such, but many others followed. One expression of the trend that particularly exercised Dostoevsky was Chernyshevsky's *What Is To Be Done?* (which bore the subtitle, "From Stories about the New Men"). *Notes from Underground* had been an open argument with it, and *Crime and Punishment* only continued the polemic, incarnating the tragedy of nihilism in Raskolnikov and caricaturing it in Lebezyatnikov and, partially, in Luzhin. Dostoevsky's coworker Strakhov was quick to observe that the new novel was the first to show an unhappy nihilist, in whom life was struggling with theory—and the observation takes particular point against the contention of Chernyshevsky's hero Lopukhov that "a theory should be in its nature cold" and that "the mind should judge about things coldly."[13] The story of Raskolnikov is Dostoevsky's answer by extrapolation to this notion.

Theory entered by another door as well. One of the calligraphic exercises in Dostoevsky's notebooks for *Crime and Punishment* consists of three carefully traced names: "Napoleon, Julius Caesar, Rachel." Whatever the last may mean, the first two are traceable to one of the sensations of early 1865, a book propounding the question of the role and rights of "extraordinary natures" that was widely discussed in the Western and Russian press—Louis Napoleon's *Histoire de Jules César.* It appeared in Paris in March and was already known from numerous reviews when it came out in Russian translation a month later. "When extraordinary deeds testify to a high genius," we read in the preface, "what can be more repulsive to common sense than to attribute to this genius all the passions and all the thoughts of an ordinary man? What can be more false than not to recognize the superiority of these exceptional beings, who appear in history from time to time like flashing beacons, dispelling the darkness of their times and lighting up the future?"[14] In the widespread discussion attending this book, critics were quick to see that the defense of Caesarism was a defense of Napoleonism, that the book was not a history but a veiled self-justification. What is relevant to present concerns is the theory on which that self-justification was made to hinge, the theory that superior natures are beyond the morality that binds the mediocre mass of people. One passage from an article in "The Contemporary" *(Sovremennik)* setting out this theory has been found by a Soviet critic to match the summary Porfiry gives of Raskolnikov's own theory.[15] "Borrowing" here is not in question; rather, we see once more the close correspondence between the concerns of Dostoevsky's novel and those of the day—indicative of a timeliness that must have struck contemporary readers and intensified the impact of the book with myriad relevancies now lost to us.

One last such relevancy—a literary one—calls for mention. The early sixties saw a flood of literature, sketches and feuilletons as well as stories and novels, devoted to the city. This literature was related, of course, to the "physiological sketches" of the forties, but its orientation and tone were already different. Here was no quest for an attitude toward the city, but the expression of one; and here one finds less the personal stylistic note than a concern with reportage. The new literature was a social literature, designed to record the facts of urban poverty, disease, and misery. These works bore titles like "Hell," "Silence," "A Ruined but Sweet Creature," "The Homeless," "The First Lodging," "In the Hospital and in the Cold," "A Day on a Barge, A Night in Lodgings (From the Notes of a Hungry Man)," "The Poor Lodgers (A Physiological Sketch)," *Petersburg Slums,* and so on.[16] One popular subgenre was the description of city streets. In Krestovsky's *Petersburg Slums* a litterateur asks: "Have you read my 'Alley'? . . . Read it; it is really a Dickensian thing. Everyone is wild about it."[17] Other popular subgenres were descriptions of taverns and the dwellings of the poor. Dostoevsky himself published a number of these works in his journals; of the sketch by Gorsky, entitled "In the Hospital and in the Cold," he wrote his brother: "This is not literature at all, and it would be stupid to regard it from that standpoint; it is simply *facts,* and useful ones."[18]

In short, the whole social fabric of *Crime and Punishment,* many of its concerns and many of its figures and themes, attach to the immediate social and literary background of the middle sixties. Even the figure of Porfiry—like that of Dickens' Inspector Bucket—is directly connected with recent reforms in police administration and theory; even the title of the novel matches the title of an article by one V. Popov, published by Dostoevsky in his *Vremya* in 1863: "Crime and Punishment (Sketches from the History of Criminal Law)."[19] All these elements, of course, are either transmuted in the novel or made auxiliary to the main drama; they acquire a predominantly psychological significance and are used to point questions of personal rather than social morality. Yet their background should not be overlooked: it gives the work added weight of reference precisely because so much of the reference was familiar to Dostoevsky's readers and could be taken for granted by the writer, so that a simple allusion might conjure up a whole social context. Dostoevsky's novel was a topical one, and the very evidence of topicality suggests how solid was the realistic ballast he put into it.

In the light of all this, the transition from the original plan of "The Drunkards" to the final version of *Crime and Punishment* becomes clearer. Dostoevsky did not completely abandon the idea of a social novel, but evolved it. In fact, the seeds of that evolution are implicit in his idea of a social novel. Soon after its appearance, he had praised Victor Hugo's *Les Misérables* as an outstanding treatment of the great theme of nineteenth-century literature: the resurrection of the fallen man. This he found a "Christian and highly moral" theme, and in it, right up to the end of his life, he saw also the principal greatness of his favorites, Dickens and George Sand.[20] A social novel, in other words, was unthinkable for him except as it touched on moral resurrection: resurrection was the rationale, the rest important but subsidiary. So the story of the Marmeladovs comes to counterpoint that of Raskolnikov, and the social—which is to say, the urban—background is used to lend perspective and immediacy to these individual dramas. The question must now be confronted more precisely: Just what is the role of the city in Dostoevsky's novel?

Role of the City

Crime and Punishment is, as a recent Soviet critic has said, the first great Russian novel "in which the climactic moments of the action are played out in dirty taverns, on the street, in the sordid back rooms of the poor."[21] What is true of the climactic moments is true of a strikingly high proportion of the others as well. Add the police stations and the shabby hotel where Svidrigailov spends his last night, and you have almost all the set changes this drama requires. Where Balzac, for contrast, alternates the scenes of *Le Père Goriot* between the Maison Vauquer and the various haunts of the aristocracy, Dostoevsky achieves a grimmer and equally effective contrast by alternating his scenes between stifling rooms and the often no less stifling streets. So the book opens with

Raskolnikov hurrying downstairs from his fifth-floor cubicle, "which he rented from lodgers," out onto the street, where the July heat and "the closeness, the crush, and the plaster, scaffolding, bricks, and dust everywhere, along with that peculiar summer stench, so familiar to every Petersburger" all irritate his already overworked nerves. "The truly intolerable stench from the saloons, which are particularly numerous in that part of town, and the drunks he kept running into, although it was a weekday, gave a finishing touch to the repulsive and melancholy atmosphere of the picture" (I,1). The neighborhood is carefully specified, in order to explain why Raskolnikov's extreme shabbiness goes unremarked: "Because of the proximity of the Haymarket, the abundance of a certain kind of establishment, and the preponderance of the artisan and working-class population crowded in these streets and alleys of central Petersburg, the general panorama was sometimes enlivened with such types that it was hardly possible to imagine the sort of figure that might cause surprise" (I, 1). Here, then, assailing the nose, eyes, and nerves, is the general scene of the action, carefully and closely observed in innumerable details. If Dostoevsky has been sometimes thought to slight this background, it is because, unlike Balzac, he tends to avoid bald exposition whenever possible; instead of a preliminary scene setting, he begins with action, and the reality of the scene is built in passing, by a host of details called forth in the order of their relevance to what is going on. The setting is a function of the action. To collect these details here would be a pedestrian task, and an unnecessary one: an attentive reading even of the first few pages suffices to discover them. But we may note that distances, too, are indicated with revealing exactitude: Raskolnikov has an even seven hundred and thirty paces from the gate of his building to the huge house fronting on the canal where Alyona Ivanovna, the pawnbroker, lives; seeing Marmeladov home from the tavern where he first meets him is a matter of two or three hundred paces. These distances set up a unity of place that is not artificial. Here is the heart of Petersburg, a neighborhood that is also a microcosm. Its compactness facilitates and rationalizes coincidence, as well as the swift accumulation of the action, just as its social nature underlines the irony of Marmeladov's reference to "this capital, magnificent and adorned with innumerable monuments" (I, 2).

There is nothing monumental about these teeming streets and alleys except the quantity of life they contain. Raskolnikov wonders in a moment of reverie "why in all great cities men are not just impelled by necessity, but somehow peculiarly inclined to live and settle in just those parts of the city where there are no gardens or fountains, where there is most dirt and stench and all sorts of filth" (I, 6). Yet he himself is drawn to them, as if by an instinctive and obscure fellow-feeling that is a refutation of his intellectual theory about himself. Here, for all its squalor, is quintessential urban life, and its forms, as Dostoevsky had shown in *Notes from Underground,* are liable to be sordid. "I love to hear singing to a street organ," Raskolnikov confesses to an alarmed stranger, "on a cold, dark, damp autumn evening—it must be damp—when all the passers-by have pale green, sickly faces, or better still when wet snow is falling, straight down, when there's no wind—you know what I mean? and the street lamps are shining through it."

Chapter six of part II, from which the above incident is taken, is a fair specimen of the world of the streets as this novel presents it. Raskolnikov slips down from his room at sunset and "greedily" drinks in "the stinking, dusty, city-infected air." From habit he walks toward the Haymarket. He passes the organ-grinder with his fifteen-year-old singer, "dressed up like a lady in a crinoline, gloves, and a straw hat with a flame-colored feather in it, all old and shabby," and makes inquiry of "a young fellow in a red shirt who stood yawning at the entrance to a corn chandler's shop." Dostoevsky's account is crammed with the sort of detail that makes it a physiological sketch par excellence:

> Now he entered the alley, thinking of nothing. At that point there is a long building, entirely occupied by saloons and other establishments for eating and drinking; women kept running in and out of them every minute, bareheaded and without coats. In two or three places they crowded the

sidewalk in groups, chiefly around the ground-floor en-
trances, where one could walk down two steps into various
houses of pleasure. From one of them at that moment there
came a racket that filled the whole street—the strumming
of a guitar, voices singing, great merriment. A large group
of women were crowded around the door; some sat on the
steps, others on the sidewalk; still others were standing and
talking. Alongside, in the street, a drunken soldier with a
cigarette was swearing loudly; he seemed to want to go in
somewhere, but to have forgotten where. One beggar was
quarreling with another, and a man, dead drunk, was lying
right across the road. Raskolnikov stopped by the throng of
women. They were talking in husky voices; all of them were
bareheaded and wearing cotton dresses and goatskin shoes.
Some were over forty, but there were others not more than
seventeen; almost all had black eyes.

It is here that he meets the good-looking prostitute Duclida, to
whom he gives fifteen kopecks for a drink, observing at the same
time her "quiet and earnest" coworker, "a pock-marked wench
of thirty, covered with bruises." "Only to live," he reflects, "to
live and live! Whatever sort of life—only life! . . . Man is a scoundrel! . . . And a scoundrel is the man who calls him one for that."
In the tavern called the Crystal Palace he has his fateful conversation with Zametov in which he all but confesses to the murders,
runs into Razumikhin, then goes out to stand on the X-Bridge
to witness the attempted suicide of the drunken woman. The
sordidness of his earlier encounters had reflected his own spiritual
state; this one anticipates an impulse to suicide. He feels disgust
at the ignobility of what he has witnessed: "No, that's loathsome
. . . water . . . not that," he mutters. He goes back to the scene of
his crime, again all but confesses, and returns once more to the
street—where he will find Marmeladov, crushed by a carriage
and dying.

    The streets are Raskolnikov's contact with life; it may seem
tautological to add, with urban life, but his walk to the islands
gives the addition a special point. Here is Nature and, as might

be expected, "the greenness and freshness were at first pleasing to his tired eyes, accustomed to the dust of the city and the huge houses that hemmed him in and oppressed him. Here there were no taverns, no closeness, no stench. But soon even these new, pleasant sensations turned morbid and irritating" (I, 5). The world of nature offers no lasting solace and no way out because Raskolnikov's whole world is the man-made one of the city; there and there alone his drama arises, and there it must be played out. Theories, like cities, are made by men and their creators must come to terms with them; escape cannot remove the problem of reconciling "living life" with the conditions of city life. So even amid the sickly life of the streets, Raskolnikov finds a kind of tentative community. His own is a tragedy of the garret, and it is kept significantly apart from his experience out of doors. There his generosity comes instinctively into play, in his quixotic attempt to save the seduced and drunken girl from her pursuer, in his disinterested gift of money to Duclida, in his helping the injured Marmeladov and lavishness to his family; and there, too, if a coachman whips him for getting in the way, a passer-by will slip him a small charity "for Christ's sake."

The real city, in short, rendered with a striking concreteness, is also a city of the mind in the way that its atmosphere answers Raskolnikov's spiritual condition and almost symbolizes it. It is crowded, stifling, and parched. All the more significant, then, is the single contrasting "spiritual landscape" evoked in describing Svidrigailov's last night. Svidrigailov's element is absurdity and chaos. After the abandonment of his designs on Dunya, he wanders through a series of taverns to wind up in a "pleasure garden" whose claim to the title is "one skinny three-year-old spruce tree and three little bushes," accompanied by "two little clerks" who attract him because they both have "crooked noses, one slanting to the right and the other to the left" (VI, 6). Even the tentative communication Raskolnikov finds possible in public places is impossible here. Svidrigailov is chosen to decide a dispute, but though he listens to them for a quarter of an hour, "they were shouting so that there wasn't the slightest possibility of understanding anything." As his suicidal intention ripens, the rain begins: "The water fell not in drops, but beat on the ground in streams. Lightning flashed every minute and one could count to five in the space of each flash." Drenched to the skin, he goes about settling his affairs and exactly at midnight, in a roaring wind, crosses the river and wanders in a bleak and "endless" street in search of the shabby Hotel Adrianople. There, in a cramped and filthy room, he watches a sordid argument through a crack in the wall and undergoes his nightmares. He hears (or dreams he hears) the cannon shots signaling a flood—the primal chaos, the revolt of element on which the city stands.[22] Raskolnikov's symbol is aridity; Svidrigailov's is water. The landscapes in which they make their fateful moves reflect this. Svidrigailov goes out to kill himself (as Dostoevsky had originally planned for Raskolnikov to do). In a thick mist, he walks along a "slippery dirty wooden sidewalk," "picturing the waters . . . which had risen high during the night, Petrovsky Island, the wet paths, the wet grass, the wet trees and bushes and at last the very bush [under which he plans to kill himself]." The streets are empty (Raskolnikov never encounters empty streets); the houses look "despondent and dirty." "A dirty, shivering dog" crosses his path "with its tail between its legs." In such a setting, he chooses a sour-faced Jewish doorman wearing an incongruous "Achilles helmet" as witness of his suicide, and with him he holds his last, absurd human conversation. They stare at each other for a long moment. Then "Achilles" breaks the silence with his caricatured Russian:

"Vot you vont here?"
"Nothing at all, my friend," replied Svidrigailov. "Good morning!"
"Dis ain't no place."
"I'm leaving for foreign parts, my friend."
"Foreign parts?"
"To America."
"To America?"
Svidrigailov took out the revolver and cocked it. Achilles raised his eyebrows.
"Vot's diss? Dese chokes [jokes] ain't no place here."

"And why not, pray?"

"Chust becoss it ain't de place."

"Well, friend, it makes no difference to me. The place is good enough. If they ask you about it, tell them he said he'd gone to America."

He put the revolver to his right temple.

"You kent here, dis ain't de place!" Achilles gave a start, his pupils growing bigger and bigger.

Svidrigailov pulled the trigger. (VI, 6)

Svidrigailov's last hours are spent on the outskirts of the city, in symbolically different weather, yet the "atmosphere" here, for all its difference from that of Raskolnikov's heart of Petersburg, is one with it in emotional tonality: it is, in Svidrigailov's own characterization, "gloomy, harsh, and queer."

The atmosphere of the interiors is no less so. From the anonymity of the labyrinthine alleyways to the secrecy of the labyrinthine stairways is only a step. Scenes of a comparable intensity are played out on them—most often of flight and evasion. The book opens with a description of Raskolnikov's creeping down the stairs of his own building "like a cat" to avoid a humiliating meeting with his landlady. On the pawnbroker's "back staircase, dark and narrow," he suffers agonies of fear as he tries to leave the scene of his crime. Staircases are (despite the confusion of directions) a kind of entrance to the underworld, linking the public with the private. They are, as it were, the tendrils of the city, half-public, half-private, uniting into great and artificial groups the various closed worlds of rented rooms and apartments. Already enclosed, they inspire a kind of claustrophobia, but the rooms do this to an even greater extent.

At the beginning of chapter three (part I), Raskolnikov awakens and looks about with hatred at "a tiny hencoop of a room about six paces in length" with "dusty yellowish paper peeling off the walls" and "so low-ceilinged that a man of more than average height would feel uneasy in it and seem at every moment to be about to bump his head on the ceiling." And the room is in keeping with his state of mind: "He had positively withdrawn from everyone, like a tortoise in its shell, and even the face of the servant girl who was obliged to serve him and sometimes looked into his room provoked him to irritation and convulsions." Here is the extreme of isolation and the fitting birthplace of his theory. His mother notices immediately when she enters. "What a terrible room you have, Rodya, it's just like a coffin," she remarks; "I'm sure it's half from your room that you've become such a melancholic." And Raskolnikov, thinking of the murder he has just committed, takes up the point. "Yes," he answers, "the room had a lot to do with it. I thought of that, too . . . If you only knew, though, what a strange thing you said just now, mother" (III, 3). Later, in his confession to Sonya, he repeats: "I hid in my corner like a spider. You've been in that hole, you've seen it. . . . And do you know, Sonya, that low ceilings and tiny rooms cramp the soul and the mind?" (V, 4). What is worse, they take on an attraction of their own: "Ah, how I hated that garret! And yet I wouldn't go out of it! I purposely wouldn't" (V, 4). Like all of Dostoevsky's dreamers, from Ordynov through the underground man, Raskolnikov "preferred lying still and thinking" (V, 4). The difference is that his dreams are rational dreams—not a substitute for the world but a plan for mastering it. "You don't suppose," he asks Sonya, "that I went into it headlong like a fool? I went into it like a wise man, and that was my downfall" (V, 4). For such wisdom his airless and sordid little cubicle is a telling symbol.

The only other room in the book comparable to this in its extremity is the room taken by Raskolnikov's quasi-double, Svidrigailov, in the Adrianople. The parallels are striking: "It was a little cell with one window, so low-ceilinged that even Svidrigailov could barely stand up in it; a very dirty bed, together with a plain painted chair and table, took up almost all the space. The walls, which seemed to consist of a few planks knocked together, were covered with worn paper, so dusty and tattered that the pattern was indistinguishable, though one could still divine the color (yellow). One part of the wall and ceiling was angled, as is customary in attics, though in this case it was a stairway that went over the sloping portion" (VI, 6). For the rest, the apartment of the Marmeladovs, the room into which Luzhin first puts Dunya and Raskolnikov's mother, Razumikhin's room, and those of the pawnbroker all share a depressing poverty, depressingly itemized, and function on the social and realistic, rather than on the personal and symbolic, level. The single exception is Sonya's, "a large but extremely low-ceilinged room . . . [that] looked like a barn; it was a very irregular quadrangle and this added a grotesque note. A wall with three windows opening on to the canal ran aslant so that one corner, forming a very acute angle, was a deep recess, hard to descry in the weak light; the angle of the other corner was monstrously obtuse. In all of this large room there was hardly any furniture" (IV, 4). The room of the sacrificial prostitute, like that of the murderer, is low and poor: but though irregular, it is spacious. His is like a coffin; hers, Dostoevsky reports, is like a desert: but even in a desert life is possible. And where his has a single window facing inward, on the courtyard, hers has three windows, looking out on to the canal. Sonya's room, like its mistress, is oriented toward austerity, but outward—toward life.

Of these streets and rooms is the Petersburg of *Crime and Punishment* made up. It is the city of unrelieved poverty. The wealthy are depraved and futile, like Svidrigailov, or silly and obnoxious, like Luzhin. Magnificence has no place in it, because magnificence is external, formal, abstract, cold. The striking scene where Raskolnikov, returning home from his visit to Razumikhin, pauses to take in the majestic panorama along the river, suggests this: "When he was attending the university, he had stopped at this same spot, perhaps a hundred times, to gaze at this truly magnificent spectacle and almost always to wonder at the vague and elusive impression it produced in him. This magnificent panorama always seemed to exude an inexplicable coldness: this splendid picture was for him the embodiment of some blank and dead spirit. He wondered every time at his somber and enigmatic impression, and, mistrusting himself, put off seeking an explanation" (II, 2). In its mysterious intensity, this recalls the sunset vision on the Neva of "A Weak Heart" and "Petersburg Visions." But where, in the earlier context, the city seemed to be invested with magic, here it is divested even of life.[23] This beauty is rare, as is the sunlight itself. The real city lies not along the majestic river but by the narrow canals, and it is closer to Svidrigailov's characterization: "This is a city of half-crazy people. If we were a scientific people, doctors, lawyers and philosophers could make the most valuable investigations in Petersburg, each in his own field. There are few places where you'll find so many gloomy, harsh and strange influences on the soul of man as in Petersburg. Consider the influence of the climate alone" (VI, 3). The real city is here, where for all its distortion there is life—which means people and suffering. Raskolnikov had bowed to Sonya, saying that he was bowing "to all the suffering in the world"; at the end he kneels in the middle of the Haymarket, "bow[s] down to the earth, and kiss[es] that filthy earth with joy and rapture" (VI, 8). "He's bowing down to all the world and kissing the great city of St. Petersburg and its pavement," a drunken workman comments. The pavement is as holy as the earth; it, too, in its terrible way, bears life.

In this scene, a magnificent touch follows the workman's comment: "Quite a young fellow, too!" another bystander remarks.

"And a gentleman," someone observed in a sober voice.

"These days there's no telling who's a gentleman and who isn't."

Here to the exalted emotional reality is added a reminder of the mundane social reality—its constant foil in this work. The role of "the great city of St Petersburg" as it existed, concretely and socially, in the middle of the 1860s, is fundamental in *Crime and Punishment*. Only once this is recognized can the significance of that role be fully and truly assessed.

Notes

1. *Pisma,* I, 408 (letter to A. A. Krayevsky, editor of *Otechestvennye zapiski,* 8 June 1865).

2. Leonid P. Grossman, "Gorod i lyudi *Prestupleniya i nakazaniya,*" introduction to *Prestuplenie i nakazanie* (Moscow, 1935), p. 23. The specific historical background that follows is taken almost entirely from this article, which stands virtually alone in treating the subject.

3. Ibid., pp. 24–25.

4. Ibid.

5. Ibid., pp. 25–26.

6. "Protsess Lasenera," *Poln. sobr.* XIII, 521–522.

7. Ibid., p. 522. Besides this introduction, Dostoevsky's hand is perceptible in the article itself, and—testifying to the impression the case made on him—the name of Lacenaire recurs in the manuscripts of *The Idiot* and *A Raw Youth.*

8. Grossman, "Gorod i lyudi," pp. 29–30.

9. Ibid., p. 31.

10. *Vremya*, 1863, III, *Sovremennoye obozrenie* (Contemporary Review); cited in Grossman, p. 10.

11. Ibid.

12. Ibid., p. 12.

13. Ibid., p. 16. The story of Sonya also has its role in this polemic with Chernyshevsky. Thus where he has his young intellectual, Kirsanov, rescue Nastenka Kryukova from a life of vice, Dostoevsky has his hero rescued by the prostitute. The theme of the prostitute's moral superiority, of course, first appeared in *Notes from Underground.*

14. Quoted in Evnin, p. 154.

15. See Ibid., p. 156.

16. Ibid., p. 133.

17. Part III, ch. 29; quoted in Ibid., p. 134.

18. *Pisma,* I, 352; quoted in Ibid., p. 134.

19. Grossman, "Gorod i lyudi," p. 21, n.1.

20. See his remarks of 1862 on *Les Misérables* and *Notre Dame de Paris* in *Poln. sobr.,* XIII, 525–527.

21. Evnin, p. 139.

22. See Dostoevsky's macabre vision of the water-filled Petersburg cemeteries in "Bobok." See also Antsiferov's observation in his tracing of the development of the myth of Petersburg from the founding of the city: "In the history of Petersburg one phenomenon of nature acquired a special significance that imparts to the Petersburg myth a quite exceptional interest. The periodically recurring inundations, the pressure of an angry sea on the daringly erected city, announced to the city by cannonades in the awful autumn nights, evoked images of the ancient myths. Chaos was seeking to swallow up the created world." *Byl i mif Peterburga* (Petersburg, 1924), p. 57.

23. Mochulsky has pointed out another side of this scene's symbolism: "The soul of Petersburg is the soul of Raskolnikov: in it are the same

grandeur and the same coldness. The hero 'wonders at his somber and enigmatic impression and puts off finding its solution.' The novel is dedicated to the solution of the mystery of Raskolnikov-Petersburg-Russia. Petersburg is just as double as the human consciousness to which it has given rise. On the one hand, the majestic Neva, in whose azure water is reflected the golden cupola of St. Isaac's Cathedral . . . on the other hand, the Haymarket, with its alleys and back streets, packed with poverty . . . It is the same with Raskolnikov: 'He is remarkably handsome, with fine dark eyes and dark brown hair, above average in height, slender and well-built'—a dreamer, a romantic, a lofty spirit and a proud, noble and strong personality. But this 'fine man' has his own Haymarket, his own filthy underground: 'the thought' of the murder and the robbery" (p. 238).

Raskolnikov's City and the Napoleonic Plan

ADELE LINDENMEYR

◆　◆　◆

HAVING LIVED in Petersburg's Haymarket area in the 1840s and 1860s, Dostoevsky observed at close hand the strains and dislocation created by unplanned urban growth. In a little-noted passage in *Crime* and *Punishment* recounting Raskolnikov's thoughts just before the murder (I, 6), Dostoevsky connects these urban problems to Raskolnikov's thoughts and subsequent actions. Raskolnikov imagines a reconstruction of Petersburg aimed especially at improving the crowded, wretched conditions of Haymarket. This passage yields insights into the character of Raskolnikov and the thematics of the novel. In it, the city takes two forms, both of which have a powerful psychological influence on Raskolnikov: the squalid reality of Haymarket and the ideal of his imagining, modeled after Napoleon III's reconstruction of Paris. Both cities, real and ideal, support Raskolnikov's motive and justification for the murder. For Dostoevsky, however, the reality of Haymarket undermines Raskolnikov's utilitarian, Napoleonic scheme of reconstruction and, by extension, his intellectual rationale for the murder.

Dostoevsky set the great majority of his works in Petersburg and made extensive use of the character types and scenes of that city. Commentators such as Leonid Grossman have pointed out the close attention he paid to urban reality and the resulting authenticity of his works for contemporary readers. Donald Fanger has argued that Dostoevsky's recreation of mid-nineteenth-century Petersburg serves succeeding generations of readers as "realistic ballast, his way of anchoring the feverish improbabilities of the action of his books in real life."[1]

The Petersburg that Dostoevsky most often portrays bears a distinct geographical and socioeconomic identity. Fashionable districts seldom appear in his writings. The classical architecture of Petersburg, Dostoevsky remarks in "Little Pictures" in the *Diary of a Writer* for 1873, "is extremely characteristic and original and what always struck me was that it expresses all its characterlessness and lack of individuality throughout its existence." The Haymarket (*Sennaia Ploshchad'*) area, however, and similar quarters of the city fascinated him. His daughter describes how in the 1840s he roamed "the darkest and most deserted streets of Petersburg. He talked to himself as he walked, gesticulating, and causing passersby to turn and look at him."[2] He often chose as the setting for a story the middle- and lower-class parts of the Admiralty district around Voznesensky Prospect and Haymarket, which in the mid-nineteenth century had little in common with the classical buildings and squares of the administrative and fashionable parts of the district. The Haymarket neighborhood, where in the 1860s Dostoevsky lived on the corner of Carpenter's Lane and Little Tradesmen Street, is especially prominent in *Crime and Punishment.*

What exactly was the urban reality of this part of mid-nineteenth-century Petersburg? Rapid, unregulated expansion in the 1860s was changing Peter I's carefully planned city and creating serious problems unbefitting the capital of a huge and powerful empire. With the emancipation of the serfs in 1861, peasants migrated in ever greater numbers to the capital to seek jobs in the city's growing industries and services. This influx and the economic and social changes brought on by the growth of manufacturing strained Petersburg's already inadequate facilities—

water supply, health and sanitation services (there were cholera epidemics in the city in 1848 and 1866), and housing. The consequences for the population were manifest: disease, unemployment, crime, prostitution, and drunkenness were widely discussed in the contemporary press of the capital.

Petersburg's most notorious slum was the area around Haymarket. The market itself was one of the oldest, largest and busiest centers of small-scale retail trade in the city. Its transient population and filth made it an ideal breeding ground for infectious disease.[3] Every available corner of the overcrowded, ill-equipped tenements surrounding the market was let out at high rents; with 247 people per house the Haymarket neighborhood had the highest population density in the city.[4] A local landmark nicknamed the "Vyazemsky Monastery" was a great block of slums owned by Prince Vyazemsky, which served as the location of the "Crystal Palace" tavern in *Crime and Punishment.* As a center of trade for the capital and the surrounding region, Haymarket abounded with cheap eating houses and taverns. Raskolnikov's own small street, Carpenter's Lane, housed eighteen taverns.[5] The overcrowding, disease, drunkenness, and immorality of Haymarket finally drew government attention in 1865, when an official commission was established to investigate conditions there.[6]

This, then, was the Petersburg that Dostoevsky knew well and chose to depict in *Crime and Punishment.* Haymarket serves as background to the thoughts and actions of Raskolnikov. These two components of the novel, Raskolnikov and the city, are closely linked. The people and conditions of Haymarket are often introduced through Raskolnikov's consciousness. For example, the novel opens with Raskolnikov's reaction upon descending from his room onto Carpenter's Lane on a July day:

The heat on the street was terrible, and the closeness, crowds, lime everywhere, scaffolding, bricks, dust and that particular summer stench so well-known to every Petersburger who did not have the possibility of renting a summer house—all this together shook the young man's nerves, already unsettled without it. (I, 1)[7]

This part of Petersburg, to which Dostoevsky immediately gives a tangible atmospheric, social, and economic identity, has a powerful attraction for Raskolnikov. The magnificent panorama of the capital city along the Neva River left Raskolnikov, like Dostoevsky, "with an inexplicable coldness" (II, 2). Even though Haymarket's stifling atmosphere and drunken crowds revolt him, Raskolnikov is drawn to it many times throughout the novel: "By force of habit, following the usual course of his previous walks, he headed straight for Haymarket . . ." (II, 6). There Raskolnikov comes face to face with the debilitating consequences of nineteenth-century urban reality—the exploitation of women and children, the drunkenness and destitution. In one of Haymarket's many taverns, for example, he hears Marmeladov's autobiography. These observations support the self-willed and utilitarian aspects of the theory developed in his article. In fact, Dostoevsky uses the reality of Petersburg not only as background but also to influence Raskolnikov's thoughts and actions and to develop his theme.

One passage in part I, chapter 6 of the novel illustrates Dostoevsky's sensitivity to the city and his incorporation of it into the themes and polemics of his writing. This passage records Raskolnikov's thoughts as he is walking to the pawnbroker's house to commit the crime. It begins with Raskolnikov, distracted from thoughts of the impending murder, lost in certain "extraneous thoughts":

> Before, when he happened to picture all this in his imagination, he sometimes thought that he would be very much afraid. But he was not very afraid now, he was even completely unafraid. He was even occupied at this moment by certain extraneous thoughts, though not for long. Passing by the Yusupov Garden he even began to consider the construction of tall fountains and how well they would freshen the air in all the squares. Gradually he came to the conclusion that if the Summer Garden were extended to the whole Mars Field and even joined with the garden of the

Mikhailovsky Palace, it would be a beautiful and most useful thing for the city. (I, 6)

These "extraneous thoughts," reminiscent of Raskolnikov's other dreams, derive from contemporary problems in the planning of Petersburg. Architecture greatly interested Dostoevsky. As a student at Petersburg's Main Engineering School in the Mikhailovsky Castle, he had studied the history of architecture enthusiastically, and this interest continued throughout his life. Dostoevsky, then, was no doubt familiar with the history of architecture and city planning in Petersburg. Raskolnikov's own ambitious scheme recalls the monumental scale and conception of Petersburg architecture and planning inaugurated by Peter I. But even the Admiralty district, the political and social center of the capital and the empire as well as the location of Haymarket, revealed the failure of this grand tradition. Although the district was the focus of much planning and construction in the eighteenth and early nineteenth centuries, most of these projects were aimed at creating a magnificent ensemble of palaces, government complexes, and vast squares for military drill and parades, modeled after Western European capitals. Meanwhile, architects and planners ignored the spontaneous, haphazard growth of the living and working areas of the city such as Haymarket, with the resulting inadequacy of services and serious social dislocation.

The lack of waterways and parks is one example of the failure to respond to problems exacerbated by urban expansion. Canals, ponds, fountains, and gardens were important not only aesthetically but also practically. Situated on the Neva delta, Petersburg was vulnerable to flooding. Waterways were essential to lessen the impact of flooding and to drain the marshy land to make it habitable. Currents of cool air created by fountains would help alleviate the heat of the Petersburg summer with which Dostoevsky opens his novel. Fountains and canals would also help in combatting the frequent fires (there was an especially serious outbreak of fires in 1862, which sparked a polemic between Dostoevsky and Chernyshevsky on politically motivated arson) and augment the city's water supply; in the 1860s water had to be brought to houses from the rivers and canals by water-carriers. Overcrowded housing made parks and landscaping for public recreation particularly necessary.

Dostoevsky is referring directly to these needs and the failure to meet them in the passage quoted above. Petersburg's waterways, like the Catherine Canal which Raskolnikov crosses on his way to the pawnbroker's house, were dangerously polluted. Despite the cholera epidemic and fires of the 1860s, little had been done to upgrade the capital's water supply. Raskolnikov's proposal to build tall fountains to "freshen the air in all the squares" echoed contemporary debates. Along with the problems of crime and drunkenness, the local press drew attention to the city's inadequate water supply; in July 1865 three Petersburg newspapers, *Peterburgskii Listok, Invalid,* and *Golos,* called for the building of more fountains in the city.[8] Central Petersburg also lacked parks. The only park built in the Admiralty district in the first half of the nineteenth century was K. I. Rossi's ensemble of the Mikhailovsky Palace and Garden of 1819–25. Built for Alexander I's brother Mikhail, the Garden was closed to the public in the 1860s. The Yusupov Garden, which Raskolnikov passes on the way to the pawnbroker's house, had been privately owned until 1863, when the city acquired it and turned it into a public park. Hardly more than an arid field with a small pond and a fountain, the new park nonetheless drew crowds of Haymarket's lower-class inhabitants in summer. Raskolnikov's plan to extend the Summer Garden to the Mars Field and the garden of the Mikhailovsky Palace would have created one great park for the Admiralty district—a "beautiful and most useful thing for the city."

The boldest attempt to meet both the aesthetic demands of a capital city and the physical needs intensified by changing urban conditions was to be found not in Russia but France during the Second Empire. The rebuilding of Paris by Napoleon III and his Prefect of the Seine, Georges Haussmann, was the most prominent example of farsighted city planning in its day, and provided Dostoevsky with the model for Raskolnikov's plan to rebuild Petersburg.

Napoleon III fancied himself a landscape architect and city planner. His uncle Napoleon Bonaparte had made plans to rebuild Paris during his reign; his nephew, anxious to establish legitimacy by his link with his illustrious predecessor, revived the project and pursued it enthusiastically. In 1852, at the start of the Second Empire, Paris was an overgrown medieval city with crowded and disease-ridden slums, dark, winding streets, primitive water and sewer systems, and treeless boulevards—conditions similar to those of Haymarket. In less than twenty years Napoleon and Haussmann had straightened and widened streets, cleared slums, constructed public buildings and parks, and redesigned the water and sewer systems, thus creating the modern city of Paris.[9]

Particular attention was paid to the creation of parks and open spaces. Napoleon III instructed Haussmann to establish "pocket parks" wherever building construction presented the opportunity. He believed that neighborhood parks would beautify the city, improve public health, and elevate working-class morality. Twenty-two such parks, planted with trees and flowers and furnished with benches and fountains, were eventually created. More famous were the major municipal parks established by Napoleon and Haussmann—the Bois de Boulogne, the Bois de Vincennes, and three large parks within the city. The Emperor personally supervised the transformation of the Bois de Boulogne from a barren promenade into a vast area for public recreation with lakes, winding paths, cafés, a grotto, waterfalls, and a racetrack. Napoleon also directed the creation of a similar park for the crowded districts of eastern Paris, the Bois de Vincennes. By 1870, Paris had 4,500 acres of municipal parks, compared to the 47 acres of twenty years before. As David Pinkney has concluded:

> First among practical planners and builders Napoleon and Haussmann thought not only of the vistas and facades of a "parade city," but also of the needs of traffic, of water supply and sewers, of slum clearance and open spaces. Here they were concerned as no planners before them with social utility and . . . they made to Paris and to city planning sociological contributions of the first order.[10]

Dostoevsky no doubt knew of Napoleon's ambitious project. Educated Russians in the 1860s followed events in the West closely. Like most other periodicals of the time, Dostoevsky's own journals, *Vremia* and *Epokha,* devoted regular columns and articles to reports and interpretations of European and American news. The perspective of the commentaries in *Vremia* and *Epokha* reflected Dostoevsky's attitude then toward reform and the issue of Russia and the West—although some positive aspects of European society were noted, the overall evaluation was critical—and cautioned against importing European ideas into Russia.[11] The May 1862 issue of *Vremia,* for example, contained a scathing attack on the adventurism of Napoleon III's regime:

> There are no obstacles on the path of the harmonious development of the internal and external strengths of the state, prosperity, well-being, etc. Is there some deficit of several hundred million?—nothing to it; posterity will pay the interest on it. Send a corps of troops across the ocean?—nothing to it; posterity will pay the interest on the war costs and the glory will be pure profit. Rebuild the city?—nothing to it; posterity will answer for everything. Now the city of Paris is taking out a new loan of 125 million francs for new works for the public welfare. . . . For these "public welfare" things an additional 139 million has been put into the budget. . . . But what do these millions signify now, when posterity will pay the interest on them, thanks to the loan system![12]

Just after this article appeared, Dostoevsky visited Europe for the first time; he traveled there again in the summers of 1863 and 1865. In letters home he expressed a qualified admiration for Paris. He wrote his brother Nikolai, a civil engineer, on August 28, 1863:

> I liked the appearance of Paris this time, that is the architecture. The Louvre is an important thing and that whole quay right up to Notre Dame is an amazing thing. It is a pity, Kolya, that you, having qualified as an architect, have

not gone abroad. An architect cannot not go abroad. No plan will give the true impression.

To his sister-in-law Varvara Konstant on September 1, however, he complained: "I do not like Paris, although it is terribly magnificent. There is much to see, but when you look around, a terrible weariness comes over you." Discussing Paris in *Winter Remarks on Summer Impressions* (1863), Dostoevsky adopts a sarcastic tone reminiscent of the *Vremia* article. His admiration of certain aspects of Parisian architecture does not lessen his general contempt for the Second Empire, especially its bourgeoisie:

> *Bribri* [a bourgeois French husband] is extremely naive at times. For example, while walking about the fountains he will start to explain to *ma biche* [his wife] why fountains spurt upwards, he explains to her the laws of nature, he expresses national pride to her in the beauty of the Bois de Boulogne, the play of *les grandes eaux* at Versailles, the success of Emperor Napoleon and *gloire militaire,* he revels in her curiosity and contentment, and is very satisfied.[13]

In early 1865, a few months before Dostoevsky began *Crime and Punishment,* the publication of Napoleon III's *History of Julius Caesar (Histoire de César)* created a sensation in Europe and Russia. The preface proclaimed Napoleon's doctrine on the role and significance of exceptional people:

> When extraordinary deeds testify to a high genius what can be more repulsive to common sense than to attribute to this genius all the passions and all the thoughts of an ordinary man? What can be more false than not to recognize the superiority of these exceptional beings who appear in history from time to time like shining beacons, dispelling the darkness of their epoch and lighting up the future?

The leading newspapers in Russia's two capitals, *Sankt-Peterburgskie Vedomosti* and *Moskovskie Vedomosti,* published translations of Napoleon's preface in February; reviews and debates soon filled other periodicals.[14]

Dostoevsky drew upon Napoleon III, especially his justification of Caesar, Napoleon Bonaparte, and himself in his book, for the character of Raskolnikov and his theory of the exceptional man, standing above ordinary laws and morality. The third notebook for *Crime and Punishment* confirms this influence in the note: "Porfiry, NB. 'Tell me, is the article in *Vedomosti* yours? Did you study it or write it [*ili uchit'sia, ili pisat'*]?' "[15] Dostoevsky also incorporated Napoleon III's reconstruction of Paris into the novel as the source of Raskolnikov's plan to rebuild Petersburg, and thus linked Napoleon and Raskolnikov again. While on his way to commit the murder, which his theory justifies, Raskolnikov develops the theory further. Emulating Napoleon III, he devises a plan for a city both beautiful and useful. His plan for rebuilding Petersburg is based on the assumption that a rational, superior man can control and change his environment. Thus the plan and the crime are directly related: they share the same ideological foundation and draw upon the example of Napoleon.

Raskolnikov can rationalize both the murder and his plan to rebuild Petersburg in the same terms, for they serve similar ends. The crime is conceived as a means to improve the lives of himself, his family, even the whole of mankind, while his plan for a reconstructed Petersburg has as its object the improvement of the lives of Haymarket's inhabitants. One probable result of his plan, for example, would be to channel currents of cooler, fresher air around Haymarket by building fountains around the city, much in the same way that Napoleon built his pocket parks. Such fountains could serve other useful ends, such as supplying water for consumption and fire-fighting, as well as beautifying the city. Raskolnikov's plan would also provide Haymarket's inhabitants with a large park like Napoleon's great municipal parks, a need which the Yusupov Garden failed to meet. Since Haymarket, with its strange power of attraction, is the center of Petersburg for Raskolnikov, he not surprisingly devises a plan that satisfies some of the needs of this most wretched part of the city.

Raskolnikov's scheme to rebuild Petersburg, based on the same principles of utilitarianism and superior will that underlie the crime, should have buttressed his conviction that the murder is justifiable. But his train of thought suddenly shifts, and the passage continues:

> Suddenly here he became interested in just why, in all big cities, people lived and settled not solely by necessity, but by some particular inclination, in just those parts of the city where there was dirt and stench and all kinds of squalor. Then he was reminded of his own walks around Haymarket, and for a moment he awoke [*ochnulsia*]. "What nonsense," he thought. "No, better not to think of anything at all!"
>
> "So, truly, those being led to execution fix their thoughts on every object which they meet on the way," flashed through his mind, but only flashed like lightning; he himself extinguished this thought as soon as possible. . . . (I, 6)

The inhabitants of Petersburg and "all big cities" seem indifferent to the kind of rational improvements in their surroundings that Raskolnikov has just been planning for them. Their indifference and their irrational "inclination" to live in the squalid parts of the city seem to undermine his plan to rebuild it. Raskolnikov then recalls how he himself has been drawn many times to Haymarket for no particular reason. Indeed, the crime he is about to commit is the result not of rational will but of just such an accidental walk. The previous day, after dreaming of peasants killing a mare, Raskolnikov renounced his plan for the murder; but instead of going directly home, he was drawn again to Haymarket, where Lizaveta's overheard remarks provided him with the opportunity to commit the crime. The next words—"and for a moment he awoke"—are elliptical. What they may represent is Raskolnikov's momentary realization that he is no Napoleon, and that if his Napoleonic, utilitarian scheme for rebuilding the city is undermined by the behavior of Haymarket's inhabitants and his own irrational actions, then his Napoleonic, utilitarian rationale for the murder may be in question as well.

By now, however, Raskolnikov has almost reached the pawnbroker's house, and his momentary awakening gives way to the dominant Napoleonic motive. He emphatically rejects the entire train of thought, especially the implications that question his original justification for the crime: " 'What nonsense,' he thought. 'No, better not to think of anything at all.' "

In this interpretation Raskolnikov's thoughts just prior to the murder underscore the importance of the Napoleon figure and principle in his thinking, and the influence upon him of contemporary developments in Western Europe—in this case, Napoleon's reconstruction of Paris. He emerges as a young man representative of his decade, when educated Russians paid close attention to ideas and changes in Europe, and Russia itself was undergoing fundamental reforms. The attraction of Europe for Raskolnikov is a basic element of his character and thought. It leads him to various mistaken ideas, among them the rebuilding of Petersburg, as well as the theory justifying the murder.

Moreover, this passage affirms the important role of the city in Dostoevsky's novelistic technique, even more important than previous commentators have suggested. The city serves as more than background. Dostoevsky was highly sensitive to the two forms a city could take: the grim reality of nineteenth-century urban conditions, like those of Haymarket, but also the city as an abstraction, like the Petersburg of Peter I or the Paris of Napoleon III. He uses the dialectic of these two forms of the city in the early passage in *Crime and Punishment* analyzed here. As an abstraction, the city reinforces Raskolnikov's theory of superior will and utilitarian action. But Raskolnikov also perceives the irrational reality of Petersburg, which complicates his theory and purpose—even leading him to a fleeting realization of his error. In Raskolnikov, Dostoevsky shows how the city, working as ideal and reality, has a direct psychological impact upon ideas and actions.

Notes

1. Donald Fanger, *Dostoevsky and Romantic Realism* (Chicago, 1967), p. 134.

2. Aimée Dostoyevsky, *Fyodor Dostoyevsky, A Study* (London, 1921), p. 49

3. Akademiia nauk SSSR, Institut istorii, *Ocherki istorii Leningrada,* vol. 2 (Moscow-Leningrad. 1957), p. 147.

4. Reginald E. Zelnik, *Labor and Society in Tsarist Russia: The Factory Workers of St. Petersburg, 1855-1870* (Stanford, 1971), p. 242; see also James Bater, *St. Petersburg: Industrialization and Change* (London, 1976).

5. E. Sarukhanian. *Dostoevskii v Peterburge* (Leningrad, 1970), p. 164.

6. Zelnik, p. 58.

7. F. M. Dostoevskii, *Polnoe sobranie sochinenii v tridtsati tomakh,* vol. 6 (Leningrad. 1973). All further quotations from *Crime and Punishment* refer to this edition.

8. Editors' note in Dostoevskii, *Prestuplenie i nakazanie,* "Literaturnye pamiatniki" edition, ed. L. D. Opul'skaia and G. F. Kogan (Moscow, 1970), p. 741, and in *Polnoe sobranie sochinenii,* vol. 7 (Leningrad, 1973), p. 333.

9. See David H. Pinkney, *Napoleon III and the Rebuilding of Paris* (Princeton, 1972).

10. Ibid., p. 221.

11. For discussion of Dostoevsky's journalism see V. S. Nechaeva, *Zhurnal M. M. i F. M. Dostoevskikh "Vremia," 1861–1863* (Moscow, 1972) and idem, *Zhurnal M. M. i F. M. Dostoevskikh "Epokha," 1864–1865* (Moscow, 1975).

12. "Politicheskoe obozrenie," *Vremia,* May 1862, p. 6.

13. *Polnoe sobranie sochinenii,* vol. 5 (Leningrad, 1973), pp. 93–94.

14. F. I. Evnin, "Roman *Prestuplenie i nakazanie,*" *Tvorchestvo F. M. Dostoevskogo,* ed. N. Stepanov (Moscow, 1959), p. 154.

15. I. I. Glivenko, ed., *Iz arkhiva F. M. Dostoevskogo: "Prestuplenie i nakazanie,"* *Neizdannye materialy* (Moscow–Leningrad, 1931), p. 196.

Crime and Punishment

EDWARD WASIOLEK

◆ ◆ ◆

T HERE IS in *Crime and Punishment* a little of everything that
Dostoevsky had experimented with in the forties and the
early sixties: character types, Gothic elements, sentimental situations, social elements. Luzhin, for instance, is not much different
from Yulian Mastakovich of *The Christmas Tree and the Wedding,* or
from Mme. M's husband of *The Little Hero.* He calculates his marriage to Dunia in the same cold-blooded way that Yulian had
calculated the little girl's dowry on his fingers. Sonia resembles
the prostitute Liza in *Notes from the Underground*; Marmeladov resembles the self-dramatizing buffoon *Polzunkov* and the suffering drunk
Emelyan of *The Honest Thief*; Katerina Marmeladov looks back to
naive dreamers like Nelli's mother in *The Insulted and the Injured*; and
even Porfiry is anticipated in the sleuthing of Ivan Petrovich in
The Insulted and the Injured and of Yaroslav Ilych of *The Landlady.* But
under the pressure of the dialectic that is brought to maturity in
the *Notes,* many of the elements are transformed.

The gothic elements that had appeared in *The Landlady, Netochka
Nezvanova,* and *The Insulted and the Injured* are a case in point: Svidri-

gaylov and Alyona Ivanovna are not far removed from the conventional villains of the gothic novel, yet both are raised to profound moral significance. Svidrigaylov has flaxen hair, pale blue
eyes, red lips, and a masklike face; he carouses in the dens of the
city, seduces young girls, and mysterious crimes are reported
about him. He embodies all the artifice and melodrama of the
gothic villain, but he is also something more. As Raskolnikov's
double and as the bronze man who can commit crimes without
feeling any pangs of conscience, the terror and mystery which
was artifice and melodrama become, at least in part, the terror
and mystery of the will and the moral nature of man.

Alyona Ivanovna has sharp evil eyes, a pointed nose, hair
smoothed with grease, a flannel rag wrapped around a neck that
looks like a chicken leg. She is not just a victim, but the kind of
victim Raskolnikov needs. For him, she represents the heart of
the corrupt society against which he revolts.[1] Her image is almost
mythic: a kind of female Minotaur devouring the prey of society
until a white knight is able to destroy her. She is "gothic," yet
she is real, and she is real because she answers to one of the
deceptive motivations Raskolnikov gives himself: the killing of evil
to do good. For this purpose Raskolnikov needs a useless evil; in
her active hurting of good lives and her exploitation of her sister,
Raskolnikov finds the useless arbitrary evil he needs. Alyona exploits so that praises to her soul may be sung after she is dead.

The Marmeladov subplot is almost a paradigm of the sentimental situation, which had already influenced many of Dostoevsky's early works, especially *The Insulted and the Injured.* A civil
clerk because of misfortunes goes from bad to worse; he ends up
destitute in the capital; his daughter is forced into prostitution;
his wife, who had come from a good family, becomes consumptive; and the children go hungry. The plot reminds us of the
Gorshkov family and Varvara's plight in *Poor Folk,* and of Nelli's
misfortunes in *The Insulted and the Injured.* But in *Crime and Punishment*
the sentimental situation takes on a new significance; it becomes
a tool of moral perception.

Consider the scene in which Marmeladov and Raskolnikov

return to Marmeladov's apartment: Katerina, her arms clutching her breast, is walking back and forth, consumptively coughing; she is breathing unevenly, her eyes are flashing unnaturally as if from fever; her lips are parched and the reflection of a dying candle flickers on her consumptive, pale, sickly face. In the corner a seven-year-old boy is trembling and crying from a recent beating, and his nine-year-old sister with a torn shirt and arms as thin as matchsticks tries to comfort him. Her eyes follow with fear the nervous walking of her mother. A third child, a six-year-old, is asleep on the floor. And on the threshold, kneeling down and ready to accept his punishment, is Marmeladov. The scene is classically sentimental and repeats situations Dostoevsky has used before: weeping children, a sick wife, joblessness, a daughter in prostitution, a husband who from weakness has been reduced to stealing money from his family and to drinking from the gains of his daughter's prostitution. But something has changed! Katerina, for instance, refuses to close the door of the adjoining apartment from which billows tobacco smoke; she insists on leaving the door open to the staircase from which the smells pour in; and she refuses to open windows, even though the room is very stuffy. She *wants* to irritate her coughing and feels satisfaction in coughing up her blood. She has apparently just beaten the little boy, whose misery has driven her to desperation. It is clear that she is intentionally irritating her misery, and seeking to exaggerate it. The same is even more true of Marmeladov. At the tavern where we first meet him, he is described as a drunk with a bloated greenish face, puffed eyelids, hysterical eyes, and ruffled hair. He holds his head with his hand, the table is sticky with liquor, his clothes are awry, the buttons barely hanging on and wisps of hay sticking to them after five nights on a hay barge. He has been, in his own words, reduced to destitution by drink and misfortune. Before a circle of jeering bar bums, Marmeladov narrates, as if on stage, all the intimate details of his misery. He seems almost to caress the vile things he has done: he has lost his job, driven his daughter to prostitution, and stolen the last kopeks from his family. He repeatedly calls himself a pig. Like Katerina, he takes pleasure in lacerating his wounds; this is what Dostoevsky had called "self-interested suffering" in *The Insulted and the Injured*.

The conventional sentimental scene in which circumstances *bring* an unfortunate individual to misery and destitution is transformed into one in which the individual *looks* for his misery and destitution, and derives some strange satisfaction from displaying it and even exaggerating it. *Marmeladov has, clearly, chosen his destitution.* Five days before his confession to Raskolnikov, when the solution to all his difficulties was entirely in his hands, he was at the peak of happiness; his wife, delighted with his job, was calling him darling and protector; suddenly he throws it all over, steals the last kopeks from his children's mouths, spends it all on drink, sells his uniform, and ends up taking kopeks earned by his daughter from her prostitution. Why does he do this? Marmeladov himself gives us a hint when he says: "I am a dirty swine; but she is a lady! I may be a beast, but my dear wife, Katerina Ivanovna, is a highly educated lady and an officer's daughter. Granted, I am a scoundrel; but she, sir, is an educated lady of noble heart and sentiments. And yet—oh, if only she'd take pity on me!" She is a lady, and he is a beast—he insists on it—but it is because he is a beast and she is a lady that he cannot help dragging both her and himself down. He cannot live up to her high feelings and sublime pride. He calls her "pitiless" *(bezzhalostnaya)*. He had married her when she was destitute, and she had gone to her wedding with him weeping and wringing her hands. She never let him forget that she had been a captain's daughter and had once danced at the governor's ball. When he realizes that he will never match the dream of her past life, he begins to drink and to pursue the opposite. "And for a whole year I did my duty by her conscientiously and well, and never touched a drop of this (he pointed to the half-pint), for I have my feelings. But I'm afraid even that did not please her." If he cannot participate in her life, he will make her participate in his life. It is no accident, I think, that he destroys all the reminders of her past life: he sells her green shawl and her stockings (he has apparently long ago sold her gold medal) for drink. What he wants is to be accepted as a person, not as someone who couldn't live up to her former husband. And it is by his lowness that he attempts, and succeeds, to turn her attention to him.

Marmeladov is Raskolnikov's double. Like Raskolnikov, he has been swept out of society; he has nowhere to go and is, or feels, persecuted by society. This is obviously one of the reasons Raskolnikov feels sympathy for him and is interested in him. More important, Marmeladov repeats the basic psychology of Raskolnikov. In his desire for self-worth he hurts himself and those he loves. Unable to command the respect and admiration of his wife through good acts (hard work, position, sobriety), he forces her attention through bad acts (theft, drunkenness, and destitution). The pleasure he gets out of having his hair pulled is analogous to the pleasure Raskolnikov gets in having society punish him for his wrongdoing.

If much of Dostoevsky's old material is welded into new tools of perception and interpretation, the most important theme of *Crime and Punishment* is new. This is the sudden emergence of "crime" as the dominant theme of the novel and of almost all the works that follow.

Crime and Freedom

The dialectic that Dostoevsky brings to maturity in *Notes from the Underground* had outrun the drama of the work. The Underground Man's spiteful forays against his school friends, against Liza, against the reader, together with his ceaseless contradiction is "thin" drama for the implications of the dialectic. The dialectic implies a dreadful freedom that is contained by no values, because it is before values; and it implies a hero that is in perpetual revolt against society, himself, and God. Dostoevsky needs a theme that will do justice to his dialectic, and it is in the theme of crime that he finds the right proportions.

Crime becomes Dostoevsky's great theme, not because he had a dark, secret sympathy for crime, but because it expresses and dramatizes so beautifully the metaphysic of freedom that had taken form in the *Notes*. Crime becomes precisely the theme that permits him to wed drama and metaphysic so masterfully. Why? What is the criminal for Dostoevsky? He is someone who has broken a law and thus put himself outside of society. Every society draws a narrow circle of what is permitted, and every human being carries within him the impulses and dreams of acts that pass the pale of the permitted. Crime is this "might be" which the forces of law, convention, and tradition hold at bay. It lies in the undefined regions beyond the clear line that society has drawn about us. In those regions man's nature is unrealized, undefined, and undared. Society, like individual man, is for Dostoevsky an arbitrary power, constructed by arbitrary wills for purposes of self-protection. What is "lawful" is arbitrary; and what is unlawful, *crime*, is arbitrary. The criminal merely opposes his arbitrary will against the arbitrary will of society. He transgresses no sacred canon; he merely dares what the timid and unfree dare not do. It is only when one is free of the domination of society's will that one is free to exercise one's will A free act is necessarily a "criminal" act, in the special sense of being beyond what is permitted by law and custom. It is in this sense that all of Dostoevsky's great heroes are criminals; all of them step outside the circle of the permitted into the undefined region of the unpermitted.

Where did the theme of crime come from? The suddenness with which it bursts upon Dostoevsky's world, as well as the completeness with which crime dominates his themes, is puzzling. Dostoevsky is interested in crime before writing *Crime and Punishment*—after all he spent four years in prison—but there is almost no exploitation of the theme in his previous works. Except for the autobiographical *The House of the Dead*, there is almost nothing. In *The Landlady*, we have the rumored crimes of Katya and Murin, and the symbolic crime of Ordynov against Murin. In *The Insulted and the Injured*, we have the unofficial crimes of exploitation by Valkovsky of Nelli's mother; and there is finally the column on criminal news of Paris life that Dostoevsky writes for *Time* early in the sixties.[2] This is pretty meager preparation for the sudden emergence of this major theme.

It is too little. But if we take crime less legalistically and if we see it, as Dostoevsky understands it, as a protest against what is fixed and defined, then the impulse to crime is everywhere in his early works. Crime is already in the Underground Man's hurt of Liza, and it is in the impulses of Golyadkin. The anticipatory resemblances of Golyadkin to Raskolnikov are striking. Golyadkin is convinced that he is a victim of the plots and intrigues of his fellow workers; Raskolnikov is convinced that he is a victim of the unjust and arbitrary power of society. Golyadkin dreams of a beautiful Golyadkin who will be born if he can outwit his enemies; Raskolnikov dreams of a superior Raskolnikov who will be born when he defies and outwits society. The frantic desire of Golyadkin to be someone else becomes the methodical plan and act of Raskolnikov to be someone else (a superior Raskolnikov). Golyadkin reduces his enemies to ashes in thought; Raskolnikov kills his enemy in cold blood. The "aberration" that Golyadkin carries off to the madhouse is in Raskolnikov turned loose on society. Protest against one's place in society becomes the supreme protest of crime against the idea of society itself. Crime does not appear until Dostoevsky's dialectic requires it: when freedom in its protest against everything fixed in society and the universe makes its appearance in the *Notes,* crime and sin burst on Dostoevsky's world as the most dramatic embodiment of the theme. Raskolnikov's crime is his free act. In the *Notes* the Underground Man had reasoned out the terrifying consequences of being unfree; in *Crime and Punishment* Raskolnikov acts out the terrifying consequences of being free.

Raskolnikov

From the first lines Raskolnikov is moving toward the crime. We meet him on the staircase: he slinks past the open kitchen where his landlady is with her humiliating demands for payment, goes out onto the hot, smelly summer streets, and then on to the rehearsal for the crime. For more than a month he has lain for whole days in his closet-like room, crushed by poverty, badgered by his landlady, eaten up by an idea that hovers like a tempting nightmare about the fringes of his belief. From the first lines we have a sense of "something having to give," and Dostoevsky plays upon this tension unabashedly. What has to be done has been incubating in his mind for more than a month, first only as a tempting flicker, then as a half possibility, and finally as a half-believed rehearsal. On the way to rehearse the crime, he has already measured off the steps to Alyona Ivanovna's house, studied the staircase, traced out the habits of the caretakers, and taken note of the layout. Dostoevsky uses the popular technique of giving the reader the criminal's intention and preparations so that he can, for suspense, play off what the criminal does against what he has prepared. He frankly exploits a "will-it-happen-and-will-he-get-away-with-it-if-it-happens" situation. Almost every detail contributes to the suspense: the lucky break of overhearing that Lizaveta will not be home at seven the next day, the unlucky break of oversleeping and of finding Nastasya in the kitchen, the lucky break of the caretaker being absent and of the haywagon shielding his entrance into Alyona Ivanovna's building; after the murder the unlucky break of Koch's and Pestryakov's arrival when he is ready to leave, the unlucky break of their returning when he has started down the stairs, and the lucky break of the second-floor apartment being vacant. Throughout, Dostoevsky plays upon the most elemental springs of suspense: alarm and relief. The murder scene itself is a classic in technique from beginning to end. Raskolnikov has to ring three times, and for him and the reader there is acute tension between each ring. Before the third ring, Raskolnikov puts his ear to the door and has the sensation of Alyona putting her ear to the door also: murderer and victim sense each other's presence through the partition. When Alyona Ivanovna opens the door a crack, only her eyes are seen; and there is the suspense of not knowing whether she will let him in or not. Then there is the excruciating moment when she turns to the light to untie the string of the pledge, and Raskolnikov realizes—as he slips the hatchet out of its loop—that it would have to be then or never. Perhaps more than anything, the tension and drama of Raskolnikov's half-conscious rummagings during the murder come from Dostoevsky's use of sound, or rather from the lack of it. The windows are closed, and nothing is heard from the landing. There is only the dull sound of the axe falling on Alyona Ivanovna's head and her weak cry, the faint cry of Lizaveta, the sound of the keys, and the sound of Raskolnikov's heavy breathing. The murder takes place in a ghastly pantomime that throws into relief both the sound of the murder weapon and the sound of the keys. The scene ends with Saturday matinee thriller gestures: Koch and Pestryakov pull at the door; Raskolnikov, with two murdered women and a pool of blood behind him, watches the hook of the door bob up and down.

But no matter how skillfully done, such techniques touch only the superficial layers of our minds and feelings. If there were only this level, *Crime and Punishment* might be an interesting, surely an entertaining book, but it would not be a great book. However, *Crime and Punishment* is a great novel, and part of its greatness comes from a technique that assaults the reader's intellectual complacency and challenges him to continual refinement of understanding. Whenever the reader begins to relax into what he thinks he understands and can accept, Dostoevsky introduces some fact, some scene that contradicts what the reader expects and forces him to rethink the novel. The reader is constantly being challenged by Dostoevsky to reappraise what he has already concluded.

The reader quickly sees, for instance, that there is more to the crime than the murder, and thus more than the suspense of "Will he do it?" and "Will he get away with it?" He sees that the crime has a social significance. Our sympathy is drawn toward Raskolnikov: he is poor and unable to continue his studies; his mother is ruining herself for him; his sister is being forced into voluntary prostitution by marrying Luzhin for his sake; he is young and talented, but for lack of money, his talent is wasted. And as he reminds us, there are thousands like him in St. Petersburg. On the other hand, the old hag Alyona Ivanovna, useless to everyone, lies in her lair like some spider, sucking out the blood of the best of Russian youth so as to erect some lasting monument to herself and to her soul after death. It is only a step from these considerations to the explicit justification of the crime as the "humanitarian" exchange of one worthless life for a thousand useful lives. The motive of economic necessity (no job, the economic plight of his family) suddenly becomes not *necessity* but a bold claim, *a right.* Crime is put forth as virtue, evil as good. What a moment before made a claim on our sympathy makes a claim on our judgment. It is an attack on our values, and for a moment the justification almost sounds believable; and although we are not taken in, the powerful argument provokes our attention. The other important motive Raskolnikov puts forth, the superman theory, makes the same kind of appeal-attack on us, but it is not radically different in kind. Mochul'sky and many before him have reasoned these into very different and even contradictory motives, but both justify crime for humanitarian reasons.[3] The superman theory simply gives to exceptional people only the prescience to know what crimes are beneficial to humanity. After we have made our peace with both motives, we settle down to watch what is a misguided act run its course. According to our moral and aesthetic dispositions, the criminal must be pursued, caught, and punished in order to satisfy our legal sense, and he must be brought to see the error of his ways in order to satisfy our moral sense. And this seems to be precisely what happens: Raskolnikov runs, Porfiry pursues, Raskolnikov gradually sees that he was wrong, and he is caught, converted, and punished.

But Dostoevsky has a way of introducing a contradiction at a point where we feel we understand what is going on, and thus challenging us to think through our conclusions. As readers we are always sinking back into an aesthetic and moral sloth which Dostoevsky continually assaults. We classify certain situations and expect them to confirm our judgments and interpretations. His technique is to trap the reader into more and more refined explanations of Raskolnikov's motives, constantly to challenge our understanding, and to attack our moral predispositions. According to conventional moral explanations, Raskolnikov should be running from the crime, and he should begin with the wrong moral idea and be converted to the right one. But Raskolnikov, we shortly see, is not running *away* from the crime but *toward* it.

Raskolnikov wants to be caught. He commits two murders and leaves the door open; back in his room with his clothes stained with blood and his pockets bulging with stolen articles, he promptly falls asleep and sleeps until two o'clock the next day—with the door unlatched! When he is summoned to the police station the following day he faints at precisely the moment when suspicion may fall on him. He had come fearing that the summons had to do with the crime and learns that it has to do with his failure to pay a promissory note. When he is relieved to learn that there is not the slightest suspicion of him, he faints so as to provoke suspicion. Later he again provokes suspicion upon himself by almost confessing to Zamyotov in a tavern, by returning to the scene of the crime and deliberately baiting the workman there (Porfiry later acknowledges that his return to the scene of the crime first aroused his suspicion), and by intentionally putting out clues to encourage Porfiry's suspicion and pursuit. In fact, the more we examine the elaborate pursuit of Porfiry, the more apparent it is that Raskolnikov has a stake in keeping the pursuit alive. It is almost comic, the way he breathes life into the pursuit, providing it with clues, offering himself as bait, and supporting it when it falters. When the scent fades into nothing but Porfiry's double-edged psychology, and when Porfiry himself admits in the last conversation he has with Raskolnikov that he has no clues, Dostoevsky tells us that "Raskolnikov felt a rush of a new kind of terror. The thought that Porfiry thought him innocent began to frighten him suddenly." After this, only Svidrigaylov is left to incriminate him, and yet when he learns that Svidrigaylov is dead, "Raskolnikov felt as if something had fallen on him and was suffocating him." Why? Raskolnikov is terrified and crushed by the thought of not being pursued; and when the last person who can incriminate him dies (Svidrigaylov), he incriminates himself by confessing his crime.

But need this trouble us? Dostoevsky had told us in his famous letter to Katkov, in which he outlined the plot of *Crime and Pun-*

ishment, that the criminal would want to be punished, presumably from guilt. Can we not see Raskolnikov's punishment as a sign of his guilt and his desire to atone for his crime? He has killed, recognizes his error, and seeks his punishment. It is not our moral anticipations that are violated by Raskolnikov's elaborate pursuit of punishment, but only our dramatic anticipations. Raskolnikov does not believe he is wrong. He believes he has a right to kill when he lies in his attic room, when he kills the moneylender, when he "seeks his punishment," and indeed when he gives himself up. Raskolnikov seeks punishment, but acts as if he feels no repentance. It is here that the dialectic can help us, for the desire for punishment in Dostoevsky's metaphysic need not be redemptive. The meetings between Raskolnikov and Sonia in the second half of the novel illustrate brilliantly the dialectical nature of Dostoevsky's world.

Raskolnikov visits Sonia twice, first to rehearse his "confession" and then to confess. The first visit is weirdly beautiful: the harlot and the murderer gathered over the reading of the Holy Book; the pale flickering of candle-light over the feverish gaze of Raskolnikov and the terrified look of Sonia. Sonia is wretched and shamed and pleased *(ey bylo i toshno i stydno i sladko)* by his visit. She feels herself defenseless before him. She is shamed at having him where she receives her guests, and timid in the defense of her beliefs and hopes. After Sonia has finished reading the Lazarus passage, Raskolnikov gets up, and with trembling lips and flashing eyes he falls down before her and says, "I did not bow down to you, I bowed down to all suffering humanity." This phrase has been underlined by critics since de Vogüé as a key to the novel because, presumably, it shows a repentant Raskolnikov, one who after killing a human being now recognizes his debt to human beings. *In fact, it is but another expression of the self-willed and rationalizing Raskolnikov.* It is a bookish reassertion of his first self-flattering and self-deceptive humanitarian motive. He bows down to those who have suffered out of pride and not out of humility. We are quick to accept Raskolnikov's bowing to suffering humanity as a sign of repentance because we expect the criminal to have a change of heart, and especially because we expect such a change of heart to take place under the influence of the Bible. But if we read carefully, we see how the dramatic situation contradicts our conventional expectations.

Raskolnikov does his best in this visit to provoke in Sonia the kind of revolt against society that he himself has carried on. He starts out—before the reading of the Lazarus passage—by cruelly insisting on the desperate and hopeless fate that awaits Katerina, Sonia, and especially the children. Katerina will die, and the children will have to share Sonia's terrible life, or at best Sonia will get sick, and Katerina will have to go begging in the street, bang her head against stone and die. The children will have nowhere to go, and Polya will end up a prostitute like Sonia. Without mercy he tears one illusion after another from Sonia, attacking even her most precious protection, her belief in God. He does this by suggesting with malicious joy that God does not exist. It is at this point that he inconsequently asks her to read Lazarus. He listens to the reading of Lazarus, not because he has changed or is changing, but because he is fascinated that someone in such a hopeless position should be buoyed up by something so odd. After the reading, he calls upon her to follow him, because both of them are "damned." But the road he calls her to follow is his, and not hers. He repeats what he said at the beginning: it is folly to cry like children that God will not permit terrible things to happen. In answer to Sonia's agonized cry as to what is to be done, he answers: "What's to be done? We have to break what must be broken once and for all—that's what must be done; and we must take the suffering upon ourselves. What? You don't understand? You'll understand later. Freedom and power—power above all. Power over all trembling creatures and over the anthill. That's our goal." It is his suffering, and not hers, he offers. And his suffering is a suffering of pride and will; it is a suffering of "power over all trembling creatures and over the anthill."

In his second visit to her, he confesses; but before he confesses he makes explicit what he had done in the first visit. In his first visit he had asked her to follow his path by proving to her how hopeless her own path (faith in God) was. In his second visit he puts the choice of his way of life to her openly. He asks her, hypothetically, to "kill" to do "good." Both have come from the funeral dinner, where Luzhin had, from petty revenge, tried to ruin Sonia and the Marmeladov family. Raskolnikov asks Sonia: "Suppose this were suddenly left up to you—I mean, whether he or they should go on living, whether, that is, Luzhin should live and go on doing wicked things or Mrs. Marmeladov should die. How would you decide which of the two should die? I ask you." Sonia answers as only she can—that it is not up to her to decide who is to live. Once again, as in the first visit, he changes suddenly from torturer to supplicant. He asks her to forgive him and then confesses. But the confession is no more than the "bowing down to suffering humanity" a sign of repentance. After he has finished, Sonia cries out in terrified compassion that they will go to prison together, and he replies, a hateful and arrogant smile playing on his lips, "I, Sonia, may not want to go to prison." And after Sonia calls upon him to "take suffering upon him and by suffering redeem himself," he answers: "How am I guilty before them? Why should I go? What will I say to them? Why, the whole thing's an illusion. They themselves are destroying people by the million and look on it as a virtue. They're knaves and scoundrels, Sonia. I won't go." Later, he will say the same thing on the eve of confessing to the authorities when he comes to take leave of Dunia and when she reminds him that he has shed blood. He answers with impatience: "Which all men shed . . . which flows and has always flowed in cataracts, which men pour out like champagne, and for which men are crowned in the Capital and afterwards called the benefactors of mankind." And he adds a few minutes later, "Never, never have I understood why what I did was a crime. Never, never have I been stronger and more convinced than now."

To be sure, he had committed a crime; he had stepped over the line of the permitted, but that line had been traced arbitrarily by those who had power. The criminal breaks only arbitrary laws, and with daring and strength enough he can make his own laws. He is consequently violating nothing but the wills of others, doing only what society itself has always done. His crime was, therefore, according to the rules of society; liberated from fear and habit, he had a perfect right to commit a crime. With clear logic, he acknowledges that those in power have a perfect right, even an obligation, to assert their restraint of his freedom. He had a right to commit his crime, and they had a right to pursue and punish him for it, and victory lay waiting for the stronger and cleverer. What is clear, then, is that Raskolnikov needs the duel with Porfiry, needs the pursuit, and when this flags, he needs the punishment that society inflicts on him. And he needs all this without having changed his mind about the "rightness" of his crime. Why should he pursue punishment when he is convinced that he has a right to kill? *So that he can prove his strength by bearing the punishment.* If he hasn't been strong enough to carry off the idea of his superman indifference to moral feelings, then he will be strong enough to bear society's punishment. It is not guilt or atonement that drives him to pursue his pursuers, but pride and self-will. He had committed the crime to prove his superiority; he pursues punishment and suffering to protect this superiority. Even more, he committed the crime in order to fail. At the end of Part Three, he summarizes all the reasons why he has failed, and concludes: "And, finally, I am utterly a louse . . . because I am perhaps viler and more loathsome than the louse I killed, and I felt *beforehand* that I would say that to myself *after* killing her!"

His strength in failure is not an alternative to strength in success, because he expected from the beginning to fail. He had not committed the crime to be reborn, but to fail. We have something of the same kind of process already at work in *The Double*. Golyadkin creates his "enemies" as Raskolnikov provokes his pursuers; Golyadkin knows beforehand (the same word *predchuvstvovat,*' literally "to prefeel," is used by Golyadkin and Raskolnikov) that he will be thrown out of Klara's party, that the "Double" will appear, and that he will be taken away to a madhouse; he knows he will fail, but he pursues failure anyway. Raskolnikov does the same thing for an analogous purpose. Golyadkin can keep alive the image of himself as "good," as long as he can keep alive the image of those who are preventing him from being good. Raskolnikov can keep alive the conception of himself as "superior," as long as he can keep alive an image of society that prevents him from being superior. He provokes pursuit so as to show his strength in bearing the punishment, but he also provokes it—and this is perhaps more important—so that they will be the pursuers and he, the pursued; they, the victimizers and he the victimized; they, the oppressors, and he, the oppressed. By its pursuit of him society confirms what Raskolnikov has made of it. If he can sustain the image of society against which he has revolted, he can sustain his belief in the rightness of his crime. By failing he makes the kind of world and the kind of Raskolnikov he wants.

We are here at the core of Raskolnikov's motives. In his confession to Sonia, he is explicit about false motives. He is not a victim of economic conditions, nor of hunger, nor of lack of money. He admits to Sonia that he stayed in his room on purpose and went hungry out of spite. He knows that he might have supported himself as had Razumikhin, if he had wanted to. " 'Ah, how I hated that garret! And yet I wouldn't go out of it. I wouldn't on purpose! I didn't go out for days together, and I wouldn't work, I wouldn't even eat, I just lay there doing nothing. If Nastasya brought me anything, I ate it, if she didn't, I went all day without; I wouldn't ask, on purpose, out of spite.' " And he is explicit about his real motives:

> "I wanted to murder, Sonia, without casuistry, to murder for my own sake, for myself alone! I didn't want to lie about it even to myself. It wasn't to help my mother I did the murder—that's nonsense—I didn't do the murder to gain wealth, and power and to become a benefactor of mankind. Nonsense! I simply did it. I did the murder for myself, for myself alone, and whether I became a benefactor to others, or spent my life like a spider catching men in my web and sucking the life out of men, I couldn't have cared at that moment. And it was not the money I wanted, Sonia, when I did it. It was not so much the money, I wanted, but something else. I know it all now. Understand me! Perhaps I should never have committed a murder again, if I followed the same road. It was something else I wanted to find out,

it was something else that led me on: I had to find out then, and as quickly as possible, whether I was a louse like the rest or a man. Whether I can step over or not. . . . Whether I am some trembling creature or whether I have the *right*. . . ."

To kill, of course, as Sonia cries out. Raskolnikov killed the moneylender for himself, and for himself alone. This has apparently been too bare and simple a motive for critics who have busied themselves looking for Raskolnikov's motives in incest, homosexuality, and earth mothers. In the context of Dostoevsky's metaphysic, "for himself alone" is a profound statement, pointing to the self's capacity to exercise its freedom and power without limit. He killed to see whether or not he had the right to step across: step across what? Obviously, the conventional (and to him arbitrary) line of right and wrong, where he can make his own right and wrong. Raskolnikov kills to prove that he is free, and if anything—including the taking of another's life—is interdicted, then he is not free. Raskolnikov fails because he did not have the courage to kill with indifference, because he chose the most "useless" member of society when he should need no reasons to kill; and because he suspected beforehand that he would not be able to kill indifferently. He does the act anyway so as to confirm his weakness and turn it into strength by giving the reason for his failure to society and thus keeping inviolate his superiority.

But it is all a mad drama of the self making its own reality to fit its dream of itself, and in the face of failure, remaking reality with the failure. In Dostoevsky's metaphysic this remaking of reality illustrates the self's capacity for endless self-justification, its ability to seize with endless refinement upon anything to impose its own image on the world and to support its own belief of itself. Raskolnikov kills the old pawnbroker, visits pain and punishment upon himself, and finally confesses so that he can justify his own rightness and destroy any suggestion of his wrongness. This explains his vicious reaction, even in prison, to any suggestion of another kind of Raskolnikov. According to his theory he should be insensitive to what he does, indifferent to the fate of others, and sublimely content to be proud and independent. But he is not: he takes the drunken Marmeladov home, leaves money out of pity for Mrs. Marmeladov, feels compassion for the young girl on the boulevard who had just been raped and anger at the rake who follows her. He asks Polya to love him, listens sentimentally to the organ grinder, and talks nostalgically about the beauty of falling snow. He desires unaccountably to be with other people, feels disgust for the very act of murder that is supposed to prove that there is no reason to be disgusted with anything, and falls unaccountably in love with Sonia.

But he hates this "other" Raskolnikov that erupts from some suppressed layer of his consciousness to contradict the image of himself as sublimely independent of life he does not control. When these feelings of love, compassion, and beauty erupt, he dismisses them contemptuously, as in the boulevard scene concerning the raped girl: "Anyway to hell with it! Let them! That's how it should be, they say. It's essential, they say, that such a percentage should go every year—that way—to the devil." Frequently he misinterprets these eruptions of another Raskolnikov. After caring for Marmeladov and giving sympathy and love to the dying man and his family, he feels a great sense of rebirth and exhilaration: "The sensation might be compared to that of a man condemned to death who has quite unexpectedly been pardoned." Clearly, the upsurge of life within him—a short time before he had looked upon a dead universe—is caused by the sympathy and love that had welled up within him for another person. But he misinterprets it as a pledge of the rebirth into will and power:

> "Enough!" he said solemnly and resolutely. "I'm through with delusions, imaginary terrors, and phantom visions! Life is real! Haven't I lived just now? My life hasn't come to an end with the death of the old woman! May she rest in peace—enough, time you leave me in peace, madam. Now begins the reign of reason and light and—and of will and strength—and we'll see now! We'll try our strength now,"

he added arrogantly, as though challenging some dark power.

Again and again he is moved to actions he does not understand but cannot help. His visits to Sonia, both in rehearsal and in confession, show this double character. He has, as has been shown, challenged Sonia to join him in revolt, blasphemed against her faith, confirmed himself in his rightness, and yet, though his "suffering" is a suffering of pride, he is still drawn mysteriously to her. He invites her to join him, but he is happy she doesn't; and if she had, he would have hated her.

It may appear that the compassion, love, and suffering Raskolnikov feels contradicts the elaborate explanation by which these positive motivations are corrupted by his will. Not at all. The fact that both poles exist in him at once dramatizes the most refined point of Dostoevsky's moral dialectic. Raskolnikov shows how the will attempts—and in part succeeds—in corrupting every virtue to its own uses. He feels compassion for the raped girl on the boulevard, and yet leaves her indifferently to her fate; he loves Sonia, but tries to corrupt that love by inviting her to share his self-willed revolt; he pursues punishment from some deep-seated unconscious urge to "reunite" himself with his fellow men, but he attempts and succeeds in corrupting it—at least on a conscious level—into a weapon of self-justification. But even while he is attempting and succeeding in part to corrupt every sign of another nature, these other impulses move him relentlessly—by a logic beyond his intentions and his will—toward another kind of issue. The battle is intense, and he tries with fury to kill every sign of weakness within him, or to use the weakness as a weapon of self-justification. It is not a simple matter of attempting to corrupt his good impulses and failing. In part, he attempts and succeeds. When he bows down to "suffering humanity," he is not repentant; and when he confesses to Sonia and indeed later to the authorities, he is not confessing from a chastened heart or from changed convictions. Dostoevsky knows that the will has almost infinite resources in justifying itself, but the will is not his entire nature. The will, for Raskolnikov, apparently cannot prevail against what is the most deep-seated and essential part of his character.

The pledge of another kind of logic, and of the existence of God, is made to lie upon the evidence of these impulses of compassion, love, and communion with one's fellow men. They properly prepare for the redemptive scene in the epilogue. Dostoevsky sees the opposed impulses in Raskolnikov's nature as the signs of two kinds of "logic" that are basic to the human condition. They correspond to the two poles of his moral dialectic. There is God, and there is the self. Each has roots in the real impulses of men. There is no bridge between these two natures, and man is poised in fearful anxiety with every choice between them. Raskolnikov carries these twin impulses throughout the novel; and in the second half of the novel, he confronts them objectified in the persons of Sonia and Svidrigaylov. His choice between these impulses is dramatized as a choice between Sonia and Svidrigaylov. The skill with which Dostoevsky expresses this choice in structure, incident, and detail is commensurate with the refinement of his dialectic.

Sonia and Svidrigaylov are doubles of Raskolnikov in that they embody in a fully developed manner the two impulses he carries within him. The first half of the novel is structured by Raskolnikov's visits to Alyona Ivanovna; the second half of the novel by his visits to Sonia and Svidrigaylov. Sonia, the symbol of true rebirth in faith, balances antithetically the image of the murdered Alyona Ivanovna, the symbol of false rebirth. Raskolnikov now visits Sonia instead of Alyona, and instead of death, there is birth in the reading of the story of Lazarus. If the murder is the central point of the testing of the rational principle, the confession becomes the central point of the testing of Raskolnikov's rebirth. Appropriately, since these two scenes balance each other, there is a rehearsal for the confession as there was for the murder scene. To be sure, Raskolnikov attempts to corrupt Sonia, and his listening to her reading of Lazarus and his confession do not come from compassion and repentance. But Sonia remains uncorrupted, and the mysterious attraction Raskolnikov feels for her is already a sign of Raskolnikov's acceptance of what she represents.

In going to see Svidrigaylov, Raskolnikov goes toward the destructive idea that had ruled his life in the first half; he goes to meet the ultimate consequences of the idea. Everything about this line of action is characterized by limitation and futile circularity. Raskolnikov and Svidrigaylov hunt each other out to learn from the other "something new," but when they meet—significantly near Haymarket Square, where Raskolnikov's idea grew into decision to act—they are like mirrors reflecting each other's dead idea. Sonia had offered Raskolnikov a new word; Svidrigaylov, the old word, only in grimmer, more naked terms than he had known it. Between the two Raskolnikov wavers, coming to a decision only with the death of one part of himself, only after Svidrigaylov—the objective correlative of the part—has acted out his play of self-destruction.

All of Svidrigaylov's actions, after Raskolnikov visits him in the inn near Haymarket Square, are a preparation for death, culminating in the grim ritual in the small hotel on the eve of his suicide. The hotel and its small empty room, cold veal, mice, and the Charon-like lackey are like a foretaste of the dismal hell that Svidrigaylov's fancy had accurately divined for itself. It is at this point, while Svidrigaylov prepares for death and Raskolnikov struggles with his dilemma, that Dostoevsky shows most vividly the ties and differences between the two men. Svidrigaylov's room looked like an attic: it was so small and low "that Svidrigaylov could scarcely stand up in it"; and the wallpaper was torn and yellowish. In a room that is, in fact, a replica of the small attic room where Raskolnikov's monstrous idea had come to birth, Svidrigaylov prepares to bring it to an end. End touches beginning, and, in his attempt to show the relationship between Svidrigaylov and Raskolnikov, Dostoevsky seems to bring the dreams Svidrigaylov has on his last night into correspondence—not wholly exact—with those Raskolnikov had earlier. Svidrigaylov's first dream is of a spring day on which he looks at the dead body of a girl who had apparently killed herself because of the atrocity he had committed on her body. Raskolnikov's first dream is of the mare beating, which, in the final furious shout of a frenzied peasant—"Why don't you strike her with an axe?"—is linked with his killing of the moneylender. Svidrigaylov looks with apathetic curiosity at the body of his victim; Raskolnikov reacts with furious aversion to the image of the victim-to-be. Svidrigaylov's second dream is of a little girl in whose eyes, even as he tries to protect her, he sees a reflection of his rapacious lust; Raskolnikov's, of his futile attempt to kill again Alyona Ivanovna. Raskolnikov is unable to act in his dream as he had in his conscious state; Svidrigaylov is able to act in no other way. At the point at which the ties between the two are about to be severed, the dreams, pointing perhaps to the essential nature of both men, show the unbridgeable gulf between them.

Now as Svidrigaylov prepares to meet the end to which the self-willed principle had brought him, the circumstances of the beginning of the crime are recreated. As on the night when he committed the atrocity which had led to the girl's death, the wind howls, it rains, and he goes, as before, to find a bush under which he can crawl and douse himself with the water he hates so much. At the precise moment, at dawn, when Svidrigaylov kills himself, Raskolnikov—who had been wandering around St. Petersburg all night—is peering into the muddy waters of the Neva contemplating suicide. With Svidrigaylov's death, Raskolnikov turns to confess. One part of himself, the self-willed principle, dies; the life-giving principle, objectified in Sonia, remains.

Raskolnikov carries within him the antithetic poles of Dostoevsky's dialectic: human logic and divine logic. There can be no compromise between them. The English word "crime" is exclusively legalistic in connotation and corresponds to the "human logic"; but the Russian word for crime, *prestuplenie,* carries meanings which point both to human and divine logic. *Prestuplenie* means literally "overstepping," and is in form parallel to the English word "transgression," although this word no more than "crime" is adequate to translate *prestuplenie* because of its Biblical connotations. But *prestuplenie* contains both poles of Dostoevsky's dialectic, for the line of the permitted which one "oversteps" may be drawn both by human or by divine logic.

Because the two impulses of self and God battle within him to the very end, Raskolnikov's confession is at once a sign of his self-will and his acceptance of God. He confesses because he will no longer be pursued, and it is only by his confession that he can provoke the punishment and hence the image of society he wants; yet he is simultaneously being moved toward the kind of punishment that Sonia wants him to accept. The battle between the two principles continues to the very end. Dostoevsky resolves the conflict by legislating Raskolnikov's conversion. The conversion is motivated, as indeed suicide or a new crime is motivated, in Raskolnikov's character. Dostoevsky does not really have grounds for ending the conflict, and it would have been much better, I believe, to have ended the novel with Raskolnikov's confession. The confession itself is at once, as I have explained, a self-interested and a selfless act. This is to say that the confession would have dramatized at the very end of the novel the fury of the conflict, and the effort of the will to penetrate and corrupt even the holiest of gestures.

But Dostoevsky was not yet ready to grant so much to his antagonists. He had dramatized masterfully the strength and power of the self, and his very skill had increased the probability of the self's domination of Raskolnikov. But he had also discerned the springs of another "nature" in Raskolnikov's compassion, and he had set this against the powerful and cunning self-interest of Raskolnikov's nature. For the moment Dostoevsky settles the issue by nudging Raskolnikov into God's camp. But Dostoevsky will not be satisfied with his own solution, and again and again he will grant more and more to his antagonists, so as to test his belief that man can be reborn into selflessness.

Notes

1. Alberto Moravia, "The Marx-Dostoevsky Duel," *Encounter,* VIII (November, 1956), 3–12.

2. Dostoevsky wrote a column in *Time (Vremya)* dealing from time to time with criminal news. In commenting on the "Lassener" case he

explained his intention in this way: "We hope to please the reader from time to time with accounts of famous criminal trials. They are more interesting than any novel because they illuminate dark corners of mankind's soul, corners which art doesn't enjoy touching, and if it touches them does so only in passing. We will choose the most interesting cases. In the current case, the trial concerns a phenomenal man: puzzling, terrifying, and interesting. Low instincts and cowardice before need made him a criminal, but he has tried boldly to put himself forth as the victim of his age. He is boundlessly vain, vanity carried to the utter extreme." Quoted in L. Grossman, "Kompozitsiya v romane Dostoevskogo," *Vestnik Evropy* (Sept. 1916), pp. 125–26.

3. K. Mochul'sky, *Dostoevsky: Zhizn' i tvorchestvo,* Paris, 1947, pp. 232–33.

Motive and Symbol

RICHARD PEACE

♦   ♦   ♦

CRIME AND PUNISHMENT, inasmuch as it is built exclusively round one character, has all the appearance of a
monolith. This is deceptive; for the fabric itself of the monolith
is ordered according to a dualistic structure which informs the
whole work. Dualism is both Dostoyevsky's artistic method and
his polemical theme. Dualism is the 'stick with two ends' with
which he belabours the radicals of the sixties; for, in Raskolnikov,
Dostoyevsky has chosen one of their number who, like the heroes
of Pomyalovsky's novels, believes that he can conceive a crime
rationally, justify it rationally and execute it rationally. It is this
emphasis on man's rationality which Dostoyevsky attacks. The
underground man had claimed that man's rational faculties constitute a mere twentieth part of his whole being: the error of
Raskolnikov is that he mistakes the part for the whole.

Raskolnikov forces himself to subscribe to the monistic view
of human nature; he tries to believe that he is self-sufficient and
self-contained, that he is capable of acting solely according to the
dictates of reason with that wholeness of purpose which distin-

guishes the positive characters of *What Is To Be Done?* Dostoyevsky, on the other hand, exposes the dualistic nature of his hero, reveals that there is something else in Raskolnikov's make-up which runs contrary to his rationalism and which gravely undermines it.

Raskolnikov is not the whole man he takes himself to be: he is 'split in two', as his very name suggests (cf. *raskolot'*—to split). His friend Razumikhin points this out when discussing Raskolnikov's behaviour with his mother: 'It is as though two opposing characters inside him succeed one another by turns.' (Pt. III, Ch. 2.) The clue to the nature of these 'two opposing characters' may perhaps be found in the ideas on human nature which Raskolnikov propounds in his article on crime. Here humanity is divided into 'ordinary people' and 'extraordinary people'; the first category constituting mere human material for the ambitions of the *heroes* of the second category. This is a division of humanity into submissive and aggressive elements, in which submissiveness is equated with stupidity and aggressiveness with intelligence. In inventing this theory, Raskolnikov has merely externalised his own inner conflict between urges to self-assertion (equated with reason) and promptings towards self-effacement (equated with the nonrational). That this theory does indeed reflect an inner struggle can be seen from the fact that Raskolnikov feels compelled to make a choice, and to seek his identity either as 'a Napoleon' or 'a louse'. These two extremes represent symbolically the poles of his own divided character.

Ambivalence permeates the whole novel. On the very first page we see that Raskolnikov, as he leaves his room with thoughts of the murder of one old woman in his mind, is at the same time apprehensive of another such figure—his landlady. Thus from the very first the reader is made aware of the disharmony in Raskolnikov between a ruthless side and a meek side. This dichotomy is present in scene after scene throughout the novel. The behaviour of Raskolnikov is now self-assertive, now self-effacing; now rational, now irrational; now 'bad', now 'good', and his own ambivalence is both reflected and heightened through the characters and situations he encounters.

Thus, broadly speaking, the first part of the novel may be

reduced schematically to the following incidents: Raskolnikov visits the ruthless, self-interested Alyona; he next meets the squirming, self-effacing Marmeladov; in a letter from home he reads that the self-sacrificing Dunya has escaped the clutches of the ruthless Svidrigaylov only to fall prey to the equally ruthless Luzhin; musing on this letter, he sees a libertine ruthlessly pursuing a young girl who is the victim of debauchery: he falls asleep and dreams of a ruthless peasant beating to death his patiently suffering horse; he sees by chance Elizaveta, the self-effacing half-sister of Alyona.

The importance of this interplay of scenes opposing aggression to submission is to be seen in the corresponding shifts of attitude evoked in Raskolnikov himself. Thus his visit to Alyona leaves him feeling that what he contemplates is too terrible ever to be carried out, whereas his encounter with Marmeladov leads him to the conclusion that there is nothing to prevent his doing what he wishes to do. His ambivalent attitude to the suffering of the Marmeladov family is brought out by his instinctive act of self-sacrifice in leaving them money, followed immediately by anger and regret at having done so. The letter from home which throws into relief how closely his own situation parallels that of Marmeladov (i.e., Dunya appears to be about to 'sell herself' in order to support her brother, much as Sonya has become a prostitute in order to support her father) evokes once more an ambivalent response:

> Almost all the time he was reading the letter, from the very beginning, Raskolnikov's face was wet with tears; but when he had finished his face was pale and contorted and a bitter, spiteful, evil smile played on his lips. (Pt. I, Ch. 3)

In the next scene, with the young girl and the middle-aged libertine, Raskolnikov's first reaction of selfless solicitude suddenly yields place to ruthless indifference; after insulting the rake and giving a policeman money to call a cab for the girl, there is an abrupt change of mood: Raskolnikov suddenly calls out to the policeman to leave the couple alone, as it is none of his business.

The dream of the peasant beating the old nag to death leaves

Raskolnikov feeling that he could never murder the old woman; yet he has only to meet Elizaveta to become once more convinced that the murder will be committed. Symbols of aggression evoke in Raskolnikov feelings of submission; symbols of submission bring out his aggressiveness. The coin of Raskolnikov's inner realm, bearing on one side the head of Napoleon, on the other the effigy of a louse, spins in a constant game of 'heads and tails' with his surroundings.

It is by this juxtaposition of opposites that Dostoyevsky clearly indicates the divided mind of Raskolnikov on the question of the murder itself. As we might expect, this is not carried out entirely in the calculated way in which one half of Raskolnikov would have liked. Thus, though many details such as the sling and the pledge have been planned with thought, other details such as the procuring of the hatchet, the knowledge that Elizaveta would be absent, the failure to lock the door behind him—all these are dictated by pure chance. The author comments: 'In spite of the agony of his inner struggle, he could never during all these weeks believe for a single moment in the practicability of his plans' (Pt. I, Ch. 6). All these details, then, he had dismissed as trifles worthy of his attention only after he was sure of the main problem. But it is precisely this element of the unplanned, the lapses of the rational mind, which leads Raskolnikov to commit a double murder instead of the single murder he had intended. He forgets to lock the door: Elizaveta comes back.

If we turn once more to the schematic appraisal of events in Part I leading up to the murder, the conclusion may be drawn that the characters encountered can be divided roughly into two categories, and that these categories correspond to those put forward by Raskolnikov himself in his article on crime. Thus in the category of the self-assertive we have Alyona, Luzhin, Svidrigaylov; in the category of the self-effacing—Elizaveta, Marmeladov, Sonya, Dunya. If this is true, it follows that these characters may in a certain sense be taken as symbolising aspects of Raskolnikov himself; for we have already noted the relationship between the categories of Raskolnikov's theory and the poles of his own inner conflict.

This interpretation raises the question of the extent to which *Crime and Punishment* may be regarded as a novel in the realistic tradition; for *Crime and Punishment* is widely so regarded. But realism is a term which needs to be defined. If by realism is meant the exposure of the grim reality of social conditions, then it cannot be denied that *Crime and Punishment* is a great realistic novel. The street and tavern scenes showing the tribulations of the poor of St Petersburg; the two subplots, one centred on the Marmeladov family, the other on Dunya—all belong to this realistic theme of 'the insulted and the injured'. But if by realism is meant the depiction of reality purged of all fantastic elements, the claim of *Crime and Punishment* to be a realistic novel is more dubious.

But the Russian realistic tradition is frequently associated with elements of the fantastic. This is particularly true of the writings of Dostoyevsky's great predecessor Nikolay Gogol.[1] It is not that the supernatural enters into *Crime and Punishment* in the way that it does say in Gogol's *Greatcoat*, though two of the characters (Sonya and Svidrigaylov) claim to have seen ghosts; nor is it so much the fact that the novel is permeated by that sense of 'mystic terror' described by Ivan Petrovich in *The Insulted and the Injured*; nevertheless in *Crime and Punishment* dream passes into reality, reality into dream, and the supernatural always seems uncannily present even though it may be explained in terms of the real world.[2]

What is truly fantastic in *Crime and Punishment* is the predominance of coincidence. Characters bump into one another in the street or meet one another by apparent chance in taverns.[3] Not only this; many characters are found to be living alongside one another in the most improbable way. Thus Svidrigaylov lodges next door to Sonya; Luzhin lives with Lebezyatnikov, who in turn lives in the same house as the Marmeladov family. Moreover, there is the question of the way various characters appear to be related to one another: Luzhin is related to Svidrigaylov (through his wife) and is the former guardian of Lebezyatnikov; Porfiry is related to Razumikhin. Yet these three devices, which, for want of better terms, may be branded as coincidence, co-habitation and collateralisation, all tend towards the same effect—they draw the characters closer together and in some measure identify them one with another. We are dealing here not so much with the realistic portrayal of character as with its symbolic meaning.

When Raskolnikov exclaims that he has not murdered an old woman: he has murdered himself (Pt. V, Ch. 4), he is proclaiming the symbolic truth behind the murder; for his two victims represent the two poles within himself: Alyona—tyrannical, ruthlessly grasping for herself; Liza—meek, selflessly doing good for others. It is significant that in Part I, at the end of that sequence of alternating attitudes to the crime, Raskolnikov's determination to commit the murder only becomes finally established when he learns that Elizaveta will not be in the apartment with Alyona. In spite of the strength of his previous doubts, this one overheard piece of information is sufficient to give him the singleness of purpose which he needs. Elizaveta represents the weaker side of himself, and Elizaveta, he now knows, will be absent, therefore nothing can now deter him from his assignation with the stronger side of his nature, represented by Alyona.

But this of course is the mistake of Chernyshevsky and his rationalist followers; man cannot dispose so easily of one side of himself; he cannot exert one side of his nature at the expense of the other, and so Raskolnikov, the would-be rationalist, irrationally *leaves the door unlocked; Liza returns and has to be murdered too.* This is why, throughout the initial stages of the murder, Raskolnikov behaves in the zombie-like manner of a man who is 'only half there', whereas after the arrival of Liza he becomes more aware of the reality of the situation: 'He became more and more seized with panic, especially after this second, quite unexpected, murder. He wanted to run away from there as quickly as possible' (Pt. I, Ch. 7). Symbolically, Dostoyevsky has shown that it is impossible for Raskolnikov to assert one side of his nature without of necessity involving the other: the murder of Alyona inevitably brings in its wake that of Elizaveta.

It is the realisation, at a deep psychological level, of the full horror of this truth which leads to Raskolnikov's breakdown. But what is significant is that Raskolnikov, with one part of himself, again refuses to face this truth; there appears to be an unaccountable blank in his memory once he allows himself to be dominated again by the ruthless, rational side of his character. For the most part, when discussing his theories and defending his actions, it is only the murder of Alyona which is mentioned: Elizaveta is left out of consideration.

Thus he can even defend the murder of Alyona to Dunya just before he goes to make his official deposition to the police, but in this defence no mention is made of Elizaveta. Even in the penal settlement he is still convinced of the validity of his theories and again maintains that it was no crime to kill Alyona: no mention is made of Elizaveta.

Raskolnikov is first reminded that he has also killed Elizaveta by Nastasya, the servant of his landlady. Nastasya was acquainted with Elizaveta, and whereas Alyona exploited Raskolnikov, gave him little money in return for his pledges, Elizaveta, so Nastasya now tells him, rendered him services—she mended his shirts. Shocked at learning this, Raskolnikov turns over in his bed and pretends to study the wallpaper.

As we have seen, Raskolnikov's landlady is linked with Alyona on the very first page of the novel. Moreover it is at her instigation that Raskolnikov is ordered to the police station to pay a debt. This summons, occurring as it does immediately after the murder, appears almost as some sort of retribution from the grave. In the landlady who persecutes him, and the servant who helps him (and is also a friend of Elizaveta) there may be seen a pale reflection of the Alyona/Elizaveta duality.

A much stronger reflection of Elizaveta, however, is to be seen in Sonya. Not only is she too the friend of Elizaveta, but they share many traits of character in common. Both are alike in their self-effacement, their humility, their kindness. Both are 'fallen women'. Sonya is a prostitute; Elizaveta, we learn, has been many times seduced and seems constantly pregnant. More significantly, however, they have exchanged crosses and are thus in some sense spiritual sisters. Moreover, the New Testament from which Sonya reads to Raskolnikov, and which he later keeps under his pillow in Siberia, was given to Sonya originally by Elizaveta. Raskolnikov himself muses on the similarity between these two women and likens them both to 'holy fools'.[4]

All the evidence suggests that Sonya is a restatement of Elizaveta, and it is significant that, when Raskolnikov confesses to Sonya, it is the murder of Elizaveta which for the first time he has in the forefront of his consciousness. Yet not only is there a restatement of Elizaveta; there is too a restatement of Alyona. Towards the end of the novel Sonya's influence on Raskolnikov is very strong, but there is yet another, and contrary influence on him—that of Svidrigaylov. Broadly speaking, Svidrigaylov belongs to that category of the ruthless, self-interested characters to which Alyona also belongs. Unlike Alyona, however, it is not for profit that he exploits 'the insulted and the injured': it is rather for his own pleasure; he satisfies his lust at their expense rather than his avarice.

The connection between these two characters is stated quite clearly in the novel in a scene which deserves to be examined closely, as it not only points to the link between Alyona and Svidrigaylov, but also emphasises the association of Elizaveta with Sonya, and the symbolic relationship of these characters to Raskolnikov himself.

Raskolnikov, having been accused of the murder by an unknown man in the street, returns to his room and begins to turn over in his mind the question of the murder and the problem of his own position:

> "*She*[5] must be the same as me," he added thinking with effort, as though struggling with the delirium which seized him. "Oh, how I hate the old woman now. I think I would kill her a second time if she came back to life. Poor Lizaveta, why did she turn up then? It is strange, however; why do I scarcely think about her? Almost as though I did not kill her. . . . Lizaveta! Sonya! Poor and meek, with meek eyes. Dear people; why do they weep? Why do they groan? . . . They give all away and look at you meekly and gently. . . . Sonya, Sonya, gentle Sonya." (Pt. III, Ch. 6)

At this point Raskolnikov falls asleep and his threat is acted out in a dream; he attempts to kill the old woman a second time, but she refuses to die. He strikes again and again with his axe, to no avail: the old woman openly mocks him. The bedroom *door comes open,* and the mocking and jeering is carried on by other unknown people. He tries to scream, and wakes up. This is how the scene continues:

> He drew a deep breath, but it was strange, it was as though his dream were still continuing: the door was open and on the threshold stood a man completely unknown to him, who was gazing at him fixedly.

The unknown stranger is Svidrigaylov; he is the continuation of Raskolnikov's dream—the old woman who has come to life again; the old woman who refuses to die.[6] To strengthen the links between the dream and the symbol, Raskolnikov is shown as taking some time to convince himself that the dream is not, in fact, continuing. The same fly that was there in the dream is also present in the room when he wakes up, and the detail of the open door (the significance of which has been noted earlier) is a feature common to both the dream and the ensuing reality. Moreover the beginning of Part IV, in which Svidrigaylov reveals himself more fully, re-emphasises the point once more: ' "Is this really the continuation of the dream?", once again this thought came into Raskolnikov's mind.'

Not only does this bridge between dream and reality indicate that Svidrigaylov is a restatement of Alyona; it also gives an ironical comment on Raskolnikov's failure ultimately to be like them. This time the duality is a verbal one. Svidrigaylov first appears in the doorway, but then he steps over the threshold and enters the room. This act of *stepping over* is here indicated concretely by the very same verb [*perestupit'*][7] which Raskolnikov had used shortly before to describe his figurative act of stepping over; for in his bout of self-questioning before the dream he had said:

> "The old woman was only an illness, I wanted to step over as soon as possible. . . . I did not kill an old woman, I killed a principle. It was a principle I killed, but as to stepping over, I did not succeed in stepping over." (Pt. III, Ch. 6)

The musings of Raskolnikov on his ability to step over are vividly illustrated in his dream by his failure to kill the old woman, whereas the ability to do so of the truly ruthless character is emphasised by Svidrigaylov's first action after his intrusion into Raskolnikov's dream: 'Suddenly, but with caution, he stepped over the threshold, and carefully closed the door behind him.'

If, therefore, Alyona and Elizaveta may be taken to represent the two poles of Raskolnikov's own character, this polarisation does not cease on their death; it is restated in the figures of Svidrigaylov and Sonya. Thus it is no accident that Sonya and Svidrigaylov live next door to one another in the same house, just as earlier Elizaveta and Alyona lived in the same apartment.

In the murder of Alyona, Raskolnikov has attempted to assert one side of his character, but has been unable to do so without involving the other side of himself: Elizaveta is murdered too. If murder is the action which expresses his self-assertive side, the other, the self-effacing side, is expressed in action by confession. The scene of Raskolnikov's confession to Sonya is designed to form an exact pendant to the scene of the murder.

The formal arrangement of the two scenes is striking. The murder is preceded by a trial visit to Alyona, during which Raskolnikov promises to come again with a silver cigarette case;[8] the confession is preceded by a trial visit to Sonya during which Raskolnikov promises to come again and tell her who has killed Elizaveta. Both scenes end in a similar way; the murder scene culminates in the ringing of the bell; the confession scene ends with the knocking at the door, which announces the arrival of Lebezyatnikov. Nor is this all; on the subject of the confession Raskolnikov has the same feeling of inevitability that he had experienced over the murder, and there is in both events the same mixture of the premeditated and the unpremeditated: 'He could get nothing out. It was not at all, not at all the way he had intended to confess.'

In fact the whole situation reminds him strongly of the murder:

He felt that this moment was terrifyingly like the moment
when he stood behind the old woman and, disengaging the
axe from the sling, sensed that there was not a moment to
lose. (Pt. V, Ch. 4)

In both scenes Dostoyevsky is making the same point; Raskolnikov, consciously murdering Alyona, unwittingly is forced to kill
Elizaveta: Raskolnikov, confessing to Sonya, unwittingly confesses
to Svidrigaylov. Just as, in the act of self-assertion, Raskolnikov
mistakenly believes that he can involve one side of his personality
to the exclusion of the other, so here, in the act of self-
effacement, he again tries to involve one side of himself and leave
the other out of the reckoning. But the other side cannot be so
ignored; *Svidrigaylov is listening to his confession from the other side of the
door.*

The fact that Svidrigaylov overhears the confession is again a
symbolic statement of the hero's divided psychology. Integration
still has to be achieved. Even after the confession, even in the
penal settlement itself, one half of Raskolnikov seems still to be
convinced of the validity of his theory, convinced that it was no
crime to kill Alyona. Yet after the death of Svidrigaylov he does
at least round off the confession and make a deposition to the
police.

At this point it might be opportune to discuss the role of the
police in the novel. Their chief representative is Porfiry, and although it is said that Porfiry represents the new type of investigator resulting from the legal reforms of the sixties, there is nevertheless much in his portrayal which hints at something more
than a policeman. Through the insights which the 'two ended
stick' of psychology affords him, he appears to know Raskolnikov
through and through. Indeed, almost like Providence itself, he
appears to know everything. Yet at the same time he is less concerned with apprehending Raskolnikov as a criminal, than with
saving him as a human being. There are, in the portrayal of
Porfiry, strong elements of some sort of 'secular priest',[9] which
can only be explained in terms of the symbolism of the novel.

An examination of the significance of the names which the chief characters bear will further clarify this.

The name Porfiry is derived from *porphyra,* the purple cloak which was the attribute of the Byzantine emperors. The full name of Sonya is Sof'ya (Sophia), which evokes the great Orthodox cathedral of Constantinople—Hagia Sophia (The Holy Wisdom of Orthodoxy). Raskolnikov's name comes from *raskol'nik*—a schismatic or heretic. Svidrigaylov evokes Svidrigaylo, a Lithuanian prince who was active during the fifteenth century—so fateful for the Orthodox world. He may be taken as the barbarian *par excellence,* the perpetrator of cynical sacrilege for the goal of self-interest.[10]

Thus on a symbolic level it can be seen that Porfiry is the representative of the temporal power of Orthodoxy, whereas Sonya represents its spiritual power. Both are striving to bring back Raskolnikov, the schismatic, to the true fold, but they are opposed in their efforts by Svidrigaylov, the barbarian who profanes what is holy to achieve selfish ends.

There is yet another character in the novel who serves to reinforce this interpretation of Raskolnikov as the schismatic. Mikolka, the peasant house-painter, is obviously to be taken as a shadowy *double* for Raskolnikov himself. Thus not only is he arrested instead of Raskolnikov on suspicion of the murder, but the psychological evidence which would seem to vindicate him (i.e. his laughter and high-spirits immediately after the murder) is used by Raskolnikov as a means of throwing suspicion away from himself: on the occasion of his first visit to Porfiry Raskolnikov teases Razumikhin so that he may enter Porfiry's apartment laughing and in obvious high spirits.

Porfiry's attempt to play off Mikolka against Raskolnikov ends with Mikolka's false confession; and the explanation which Porfiry gives for this phenomenon is that Mikolka wishes to take on suffering because he is a schismatic—'*On iz raskol'nikov'*. The form in which this is expressed is worthy of note.

But Mikolka does not represent only the 'confessional' side of Raskolnikov. Connected with the name Mikolka is a hint of the same duality which plagues Raskolnikov himself; the peasant who beats the horse to death in Raskolnikov's dream is also called Mikolka. It is perhaps significant too that, just as there had been these painters in the house at the time of the murder, there are also painters present when Raskolnikov returns to the scene of the crime and seems driven to display his guilt.

Religious significance permeates the novel. Some commentators, for example, point to the trinitarian symbolism in the three windows in Sonya's room.[11] Sonya, too, lives with the Kapernaumov family—a name derived from the Capernaum of the New Testament. It is, however, in the theme of Lazarus that the positive religious meaning of the novel resides. Sonya's reading of the story of the resurrection of Lazarus has a great effect on Raskolnikov, and we are told that the New Testament (originally Elizaveta's) which he has with him in the penal settlement, and which is principally responsible for his own 'resurrection', is the same New Testament from which Sonya had read to him the story of the raising of Lazarus. Even before the reading of this story, Porfiry had challenged him on his faith in it, and Raskolnikov had replied that he believed literally in the raising of Lazarus.

However, Dostoyevsky had to sacrifice much of his original intention in the scene where the story is read (Pt. IV, Ch. 4), a scene which he himself regarded as the high point of the novel. A prostitute reading holy scripture to a murderer was considered too provocative an incident by his publisher, Katkov, and reluctantly Dostoyevsky had to abandon his original intention. This explains why the theme of the raising of Lazarus is not as fully developed in the novel as its author undoubtedly would have liked.

It may at first sight seem strange that Raskolnikov, who commits a particularly vile murder, should be identified with religious heresy, but the sense in which he is a heretic may be shown by an analysis of the motives which inspired the crime. Here we come up against duality once more. The murder itself, as events turn out, becomes a double murder; but the crime even in its original conception was twofold—murder plus robbery.

More significant still is the fact that Raskolnikov gives two distinct motives for his crime; on the one hand he alleges that his motive was to obtain money for himself and his family: on the other hand, he talks about the crime as an exercise in self knowledge. For the first explanation to hold true, murder is unnecessary; robbery alone would have sufficed, or even the crime of counterfeiting, which serves in the novel as a commentary theme for Raskolnikov's own crime.

This motive, however, is not quite what it seems: it is not a straightforward question of personal gain. Raskolnikov justifies himself on social grounds; the murder of Alyona, in itself, is seen as the elimination of a social evil; whilst the appropriation of her wealth has the aim of righting social injustices. Although in Raskolnikov's scheme for the righting of social wrongs charity appears to begin at home (he himself and his immediate family are to be the prime beneficiaries of Alyona's wealth), the implications behind such charity are nevertheless much wider; for Raskolnikov believes that by using the money for good deeds he can thereby cancel out the bad deed of murder. The motive is, therefore, in essence a social one, in spite of its personal implications: it is the application of Luzhin's theory of 'enlightened self-interest'.

It is the second motive, however, which is really the personal one; for according to this explanation Raskolnikov is trying to define his own nature, trying to find out whether he is a Napoleon or a louse. This motive, as we have already seen, goes back to Raskolnikov's article on crime; therefore, although it is in essence a personal motive it cannot be divorced entirely from social implications.

The social motivation for the crime links Raskolnikov with the heroes of Pomyalovsky's novels, with the nihilists, among whose ranks Dostoyevsky had already observed a schism. In a social context, Raskolnikov is an extremist and a fanatic, who when faced with a *wall* of accepted social morality *steps over* it, in order to better himself, his immediate family and humanity in general.

The personal motivation for the crime, on the other hand, points to the rebellion of the underground man, to the deification of man's will in his striving towards godhead; for Raskolnikov, in his assault on the wall, is measuring against it the strength of his own will. To this extent he is a rebel in a religious sense; a heretic who believes that the unlimited powers of godhead reside in himself. Indeed, when he is in the penal settlement, Raskolnikov has a dream of a disease sweeping Europe through which men become 'possessed', and each one regards himself as the bearer of truth. The implications behind this dream are those of heresy, and its specific relevance is for Raskolnikov himself.[12]

There are, therefore, in Raskolnikov two types of rebel: a social one and a religious one, and both are linked to schism. There is, of course, no fundamental incompatibility between the two motives he alleges; for it is quite feasible that he could have intended to show himself a Napoleonic man by the same act that benefited others. Yet, despite this, there appears to be a real sense of dichotomy in the mind of Raskolnikov himself. During his confession to Sonya he alleges now one motive, now the other. But there are flaws in both explanations.

If he murdered for money, why was it that he showed so little interest in his acquisitions both at the time of the murder and afterwards? On the other hand, if he were genuinely trying to prove himself a Napoleonic man, can he seriously equate the murder of some pitiable old woman with the grandiose exploits of Napoleon? Even more fundamental is his own recognition that a Napoleon would not have had the doubts about his actions that he himself has had. The mere fact that he had to prove himself shows that he secretly had doubts about his being a Napoleonic man, and this alone shows that he was not entitled to commit the crime.

Once more we return to the idea that the ambivalence of Raskolnikov's character precludes that singleness of purpose which marks out the Napoleonic man from the rest of humanity. Raskolnikov in his confession to Sonya shows himself aware of this. Even before committing the crime he had sensed that the weakness implicit in his self-questioning gave him no right to attempt it, that by asserting one side of his nature at the expense of the other he was dooming himself to failure. The crime, therefore, assumes the nature of an exercise in self-deception masquerading as an act of self-knowledge.

When taxed by Sonya, he is unable in the last analysis to put forward either of these two alleged motives as the real reason for the murder; he falls back on the idea that the murder is in some sense symbolic, claiming that he killed himself (or even, as earlier, a principle) and not an old woman; she was killed, he claims, by the devil. If he *is* to accept full responsibility for the murder, the only explanation he seems able to offer is that he killed for himself; an explanation which seems to exclude any rational motivation but appears rather to indicate some irrational need to kill for its own sake. In the last analysis Raskolnikov is just as perplexed about his motive for the murder as is the reader.

We have seen that Raskolnikov's failure to achieve his ends is brought about because of the opposing characters within himself. But the process of writing with Dostoyevsky is a process of the splitting and subdividing of idea cells; Svidrigaylov and Sonya, although representing poles of Raskolnikov's character, nevertheless undergo the same sort of polarisation themselves.

At first sight it might appear that Svidrigaylov has no philanthropic side to his nature at all; no other interests but the interests of self. He appears to be a man who can 'step over' with impunity. He has led a life of debauchery; is reputed to have seduced a fourteen-year-old deaf mute, and by this act to be responsible for her suicide; it is also held that he bears some measure of guilt in the death of one of his servants; and he is accused of having poisoned his wife. On all these scores he appears to have a clear conscience.

Yet all these deeds are of a different order from that of the central crime of the novel, in that the reader is given no definite proof of their reality: all Svidrigaylov's crimes belong to a penumbra of hearsay and rumour which surrounds him up to, and even after, his first appearance in the novel. It is the symbolic act of stepping over Raskolnikov's threshold, bringing him out of this shadowy land of imputation into the action of the novel itself, which marks the beginning of Svidrigaylov's growing ambivalence.

Thus, at this very first meeting with Raskolnikov, he shows that he has a human flaw: he is in love with Raskolnikov's sister; and he himself presents us with a possible ambivalent interpretation of his behaviour towards her, by asking whether he is really to be considered a monster or a victim. The philosophy of out-and-out humanism which he expresses in the Latin tag, *nihil humanum,* might seem to permit him everything, but it also makes human weakness possible—Svidrigaylov is in love.

Whatever Dunya's attitude to Svidrigaylov may be (and there are indications that she is not entirely unresponsive to his advances), Svidrigaylov is determined to pursue her by all the means within his power. He attempts bribery, blackmail and in the last resort violence, but Dunya draws out a revolver and fires twice at her would-be seducer. The first bullet grazes his scalp, the second shot misfires, and then, although there is yet a third bullet in the chamber, she throws the revolver away. Svidrigaylov attempts to embrace her, but realising in despair that she does not love him,[13] and that for once in his life he is powerless—powerless to compel her love—he lets her go.

After this scene, Svidrigaylov seems a changed man; he openly acknowledges another side to his character. Thus he calls on Sonya and confirms the arrangements he has made to take care of the remaining members of her family (arrangements which had been first mooted as part of his campaign to win Dunya). He then calls on his sixteen-year-old fiancée and leaves her a present of fifteen thousand roubles (Svidrigaylov's wealth had originally been the lure for this fresh young victim).[14]

He takes a room in a shabby hotel, which in its cramped poverty is reminiscent of Raskolnikov's room, and through a chink in the wall he witnesses a squalid scene of aggression and submission, symbolically recalling the dilemma which haunts Raskolnikov and which now appears to be affecting Svidrigaylov himself. His last action in leaving this room is a futile attempt to catch a fly; the motif of the fly links Svidrigaylov's departure from the pages of the novel with his first appearance in the room of Raskolnikov.

During his brief stay in this room, Svidrigaylov is haunted by dreams which reflect the ambivalence of his relations with women. Thus he thinks of Dunya and falls asleep to dream of a mouse which torments him. His second dream is of the fourteen-year-old girl for whose death his 'love' has been responsible, and his third dream is even more striking; he comforts a five-year-old girl who turns out eventually to be a child prostitute. The central dilemma behind all these dreams is whether the lover is a tyrant or a victim.

The night culminates in his suicide with the revolver loaded with Dunya's one remaining bullet; as Dunya cannot feel sufficiently strongly for him even to kill him, Svidrigaylov is reduced to completing the attempt himself and thus turn murder into suicide. The gun which he uses in this act recalls in the chain of its provenance the New Testament instrumental in resurrecting Raskolnikov; for the revolver is not merely Dunya's, it had come originally from Svidrigaylov's wife, and his relations with her have the same ambiguity as his relations with Dunya (in his marriage and subsequent incarceration in the country was Svidrigaylov his wife's victim, or in the circumstances of her death did he play the role of a monster?). The choice of surroundings for his suicide symbolises the nature of his inner dichotomy. Svidrigaylov shoots himself in front of a tiny Jew in a soldier's greatcoat and an Achilles helmet, and commits an act of self-immolation before a symbol of his own personal tragedy; for in the figure of the Jew wrapped up in the soldier's greatcoat, we have one of the persecuted dressed up as one of the persecutors. This idea is further reinforced by the detail of the Achilles helmet, and by the fact, too, that this incongruous figure is itself referred to as 'Achilles'. Here we have an obvious reference to the hero who is apparently unvanquishable, until his one fatal flaw has been discovered. Svidrigaylov commits suicide because he realises that the question he first put to Raskolnikov has been answered: he is *both* monster and victim, *both* oppressor and oppressed.

If the fate of Svidrigaylov shows that ruthlessness has its weaknesses and its unexpected philanthropy, the way of Sonya, the way of self-effacement, is also seen to have its pitfalls. The dark side of humility is foreshadowed in the person of Marmeladov. He is a weak, submissive character who is responsible for much human suffering; for it is he who must be blamed for the plight of his wife and family. Confession, which for Raskolnikov is the symbolic act of self-effacement, has become for Marmeladov a subtle weapon of aggression. Those who listen to Marmeladov's words of self-denigration feel more uncomfortable than Marmeladov himself; they themselves in some underhand way are being attacked.[15] It may be objected that Marmeladov is not genuinely humble, that he is merely a caricature of humility, but no such criticism could be levelled at his daughter, Sonya, yet the humility of Sonya is shown to have its dark side too.

Raskolnikov does not react uncritically to the influence of Sonya; he points out the flaws in her attitude to life. His objections are that by her very humility, by her very submissiveness, Sonya is vulnerable, and that this does not merely affect herself; for, since she is the breadwinner, her family must suffer through her vulnerability, as it had suffered through the shortcomings of her father.

Raskolnikov's point is proved when Luzhin nearly succeeds in having Sonya arrested on a trumped-up charge of theft. Sonya's submissiveness reveals itself as powerless in the face of active evil. She is only saved from prison by the intervention of forceful characters—Lebezyatnikov and Raskolnikov. The fact that Sonya would suffer is not the point. If she were unable to earn money, argues Raskolnikov, the innocent victims of her plight would be her younger brothers and sisters as well as her consumptive step-mother. Although Sonya's submissiveness in the face of Luzhin's active malice does not, in the event, have this effect, the threat is nevertheless there, and it is this incident which comes as the last straw to break her step-mother's long overburdened sanity.

But it is in a second way that the submissiveness of Sonya must be held partly responsible for the death of Katerina Ivanovna and the degradation of her children. Sonya's inability to cope with Luzhin's malice causes her to flee in distress to her room. Raskolnikov follows her there in triumph ('What will you say now, Sof'ya Semyonovna'); for he is seeking to convince himself that his own way of providing for his family, by sacrificing others, is correct; whereas Sonya's way of doing so, by sacrificing herself, is wrong. He thinks that his criticism of her humility has now been fully vindicated by the plot of Luzhin, but at the same time he also tells her of the effect that this incident has had on Katerina Ivanovna.

On hearing of this, Sonya's first impulse is to go to the aid of her step-mother, but Raskolnikov for motives of his own (the confession), prevails on her to stay. Once again, through her submissiveness, Sonya must be held in some measure responsible for the suffering of others; for had she asserted herself against the arguments of Raskolnikov and gone to take care of her step-mother, the harrowing sequence of events leading up to the death of Katerina Ivanovna could have been avoided. Even if the death itself were inevitable, the degradation imposed on the children before her death could have been prevented by the presence of Sonya, and the greatest crimes for Dostoyevsky are always those committed against children.

It is as though Dostoyevsky is forcing a parallel between Sonya's sin of omission and Raskolnikov's crime of commission, when he makes Raskolnikov put the choice to her of either allowing Luzhin to live and carry on with his underhand deeds or letting Katerina Ivanovna die. Sonya refuses to make the choice, but in reality she has already chosen; the very submissiveness which prevents her from defending herself against Luzhin, also prevents her from denying Raskolnikov's right to keep her from her step-mother's side in time of need. Therefore, because she is prepared to allow Luzhin to go on living and commit his vile deeds, she is also prepared to let Katerina Ivanovna die.[16] In the very scene where Raskolnikov yields to the promptings of his own weaker side, Sonya in staying to listen to this confession is also unwittingly culpable herself; active guilt and passive guilt are dovetailed together.

Svidrigaylov, the dark antithesis of Sonya, is the unseen witness both of Raskolnikov's confession of action and also of Sonya's failure to act. By way of stressing Sonya's culpability, Svidrigaylov mysteriously turns up at the death of Katerina Ivanovna, and by quoting back to Raskolnikov his own words on the choice between the life of Luzhin and the death of Katerina Ivanovna, he indicates in one sentence that, not only has he heard the confession, but that he also understands the implications of the death of Katerina Ivanovna for Sonya. Then, as if finally to drive the point home that Sonya's submissiveness has failed to provide a safeguard for her family, it is Svidrigaylov, of all people, who offers to look after them.

These implications behind Sonya's own position during the confession scene would seem to weaken the case for confession itself, and it is only much later that Raskolnikov makes his deposition to the police. Yet neither the confession nor the deposition shows true repentance. Genuine repentance does not come in the novel, not even in the Epilogue; it is a process destined to take seven years after the closing scene of the novel, and could, as Dostoyevsky comments, form the theme for a new novel. It is important to bear these facts in mind; for it is commonly held that the ending of *Crime and Punishment* is unconvincing, that the reader does not really believe in the rehabilitation of Raskolnikov. It is perhaps true that the Epilogue is not written with the same intensity as the rest of the novel, but this should not lead us to assume that the resurrection of Raskolnikov is unconvincing. The Epilogue does not deal with this resurrection: it only marks the beginning of the road.

To regard the hero's rehabilitation as improbable is perhaps to suffer from the same partial blindness that affects Raskolnikov himself: i.e., to disregard the 'Elizaveta' in his make-up. Raskolnikov is not morally corrupt in the normal sense; on the contrary, it is possible to compile an impressive list of his 'good deeds'. Thus, though in a state of penury himself, he gives money away to the needy on various occasions: once to the Marmeladov family; another time to the policeman to whose care he entrusts the drunken girl; yet again to a prostitute in the street. His charity is also stressed by Razumikhin; at the university he had supported a consumptive fellow-student; and later, when the young man had died, he had also taken upon himself to support his father. Nor is his philanthropy lacking in personal valour; even his landlady gives evidence that he had once rescued two small children from a burning apartment and had himself been burned in the process. Indeed one reason for his crime is, paradoxically enough, his compassion for the 'insulted and injured'.

Yet if the two sides of Raskolnikov's character are ever to be integrated there is a genuine need for contrition. The need to confess, which Raskolnikov feels, may be taken as an urge towards contrition; throughout the course of the novel Raskolnikov has many promptings to confess. Such promptings occur from the very first. Indeed, immediately after the murder he thinks of kneeling down in the police station and blurting out the truth. In his dealings with the police, the idea of confession haunts him more than once; thus to Zametov, the police clerk, he makes a mocking, false confession, and later he even feels prompted to go back to the scene of the crime, and arouse suspicion there by his strange behaviour. Yet most surprising of all is the claim he makes to Sonya, that when he had first heard about her through her father, he had resolved there and then to tell her about the murder. This can only mean that he had thought of telling Sonya about the murder even before it had been committed. The two elements which mark his divided psychology are discernibly associated with one another even prior to their expression in action. Indeed, as might be expected, it even appears that the idea of confession is, in a certain sense, simultaneous in conception with the plan of murder itself; for Raskolnikov claims that he had first discussed the possibility of the crime with another Sonya-like figure, his ailing sweetheart, the landlady's daughter, who has died before the action of the novel begins.

Although this need for confession is fundamental to Raskolnikov's nature, and has resulted in his telling Sonya about the murder and in his ultimate deposition to the police, nevertheless he himself knows full well that confession is not the same as contrition. Even when he has taken on his suffering, and is a convict in the penal settlement, he says how happy he would feel if he could only blame himself for what he has done. That he cannot do so is because, as yet, he has not managed to resolve the conflict within himself; the self-assertive side of Raskolnikov's character, although its position is now undoubtedly weaker, is making its last stand.

The reconciliation of the two opposing elements within Raskolnikov will result in the resurrection that Dostoyevsky prophesies for his hero. The self-assertive side will not be eradicated: its energies will be fused with the gentle, self-effacing qualities of the other side. A new Raskolnikov will emerge to fulfil the exhortation of Porfiry, that he must be a sun for all to see. The beginnings of this integration are discernible in the Epilogue: 'Life had taken the place of dialectics, and something else, completely different, had to work itself out in his consciousness.' The inevitability of this change can be seen by tracing Raskolnikov's development through the Epilogue.

Isolated from the other prisoners through his pride, there is only one person to whom he can turn for help, who represents something other than the hard conditions of the penal settlement; that person is, of course, Sonya. Although all the other prisoners like Sonya, there is still a part of Raskolnikov which struggles against her; but his own intolerable position as an outcast among the outcasts is brought home to him when some of the other convicts attempt to murder him on the grounds that he is an atheist. He falls ill, and in his weakened physical state dreams of a disease sweeping Europe from Asia. This dream is an allegory, which shows Raskolnikov what would happen if everybody were to set himself up as a prophet of some 'new truth'; the relevance of this for Raskolnikov's own theories is obvious.

But Sonya, too, has fallen ill and is no longer able to see him. First he realises that he misses her; then when next he sees her he realises that he loves her. This sudden love for Sonya is not something unexpected or fortuitous; the foundations have been laid long ago in the novel—it is, if anything, overdue. Raskolnikov's love for Sonya, and the echo she awakens in the humble side of his nature, is the corner-stone on which he may build the edifice of a new Raskolnikov. Through his love for Sonya he comes to the New Testament, given to him by Sonya and in turn given to her by Elizaveta. Nor is this new-found religious belief entirely unexpected; throughout the course of the novel Raskolnikov gives many indications of his adherence to Christian belief. Thus during his first visit to the Marmeladov family he asks Polechka to pray for him; a request which he repeats to his mother before he goes off to Siberia, and he asserts his faith quite strongly during his first interview with Porfiry.

His love for Sonya, his new-found religious faith, the discipline of the penal settlement—all these are weapons against Raskolnikov's pride and self-assertion. If, however, doubt is still felt on the probability of Raskolnikov's 'resurrection', it should be remembered that at the end of the Epilogue he still has seven long years of suffering ahead of him in which to work out his salvation; and the author himself had direct experience of the way the Russian penal settlement could change a man.

Crime and Punishment is often described as a 'psychological thriller'; this description is quite accurate, but it is a 'thriller' in which suspense is created not through the attempts to detect the culprit, but through the culprit's own wayward efforts to resist detection. Here the reader himself is put in the position of a murderer, and follows with a disturbing degree of self-identification the inner struggles of a psychologically tormented personality.

In this sense *Crime and Punishment* is a 'psychological thriller' at a much deeper level. Behind the story of murder, confession and moral rehabilitation lies an exploration, through symbol and allegory, of the divided nature of the hero; an exploration in which the other characters surround the central figure like mirrors reflecting and distorting aspects of his own dilemma. It is a measure of the greatness of Dostoyevsky that these characters can at the same time stand on their own; for they have individuality in their own right.[17] Moreover symbol and allegory are so skilfully fused into the narrative that their presence, far from exerting a deadening influence, or reducing the novel to a mere mechanical abstraction, enriches and further deepens the significance of the work. *Crime and Punishment* is, above all, an extremely readable novel.

Notes

References to the Russian text of *Crime and Punishment* are to vol. 5 of
F. M. Dostoyevsky, *Sobraniye Sochineniy v desyati tomakh*, Moscow, 1956–58,
indicated in the notes as *D*.5 plus a page reference.

1. The 'realism' of Pushkin also has particular relevance for *Crime and
Punishment*. Dostoyevsky was extremely enthusiastic about Pushkin's story,
The Queen of Spades, valuing it both for the element of the fantastic and
for its treatment of the inner struggles and final collapse of the hero.
(See M. A. Polivanova, 'Zapis' o poseshchenii Dostoyevskogo 9 Iyunya
1880 goda', in *F. M. Dostoyevsky v vospominaniyakh sovremennikov* (2 vols.), Moscow, 1964. Vol. 2, pp. 361 and 363.) The story, set in St Petersburg, concerns a ruthless young man with a Napoleonic profile, who plays with
people as though they are cards (so the 'realism' of the story is rich in
symbol). To gain a gambling secret from an aged countess he poses as
the lover of her companion. He unwittingly kills the old woman and
is saved by Liza (the companion). The central core of both works is
strikingly similar: a tyrannical old woman who bullies a meek Elizaveta
Ivanovna is killed by a young man with Napoleonic aspirations. (See
also K. Mochul'sky, *Dostoyevsky, Zhizn' i tvorchestvo* (Paris, 1947), p. 238.)
   Elsewhere in Pushkin we read: 'We all aim at being Napoleons/The
millions of two-legged creatures/Are merely tools for us.' (*Yevgeniy Onegin*,
Ch. 2, stanza xiv.)
2. Thus the 'miracle' of Raskolnikov's unexpected meeting with Svidrigaylov in Pt. VI is explained by the latter as a quirk of memory.
3. E. J. Simmons takes this as a sign of bad writing. See E. J. Simmons,
Dostoevsky. The Making of a Novelist (New York, 1962), pp. 169–70.
4. I.e. *yurodivyy*. The 'holy fool' is a constantly recurring figure in
Dostoyevsky's novels, and here the comparison is particularly significant
in view of the traditional role of the *yurodivyy* as the voice of conscience
speaking out against the tyrant (cf. Nikolka in Pushkin's *Boris Godunov*, or
the historical figure of Nicholas Salos, who put Ivan the Terrible to
shame when he was about to sack the city of Pskov).
5. By this italicised *she* Raskolnikov appears to be referring to Alyona
and not to his mother (see *D*.5, p. 286), but the apparent continuity of
thought between an expression of hatred for his mother and hatred for
Alyona is interesting. For a theory on the role played by the mother in
the motives for the crime, see Wasiolek's commentary to *The Notebooks
for 'Crime and Punishment'*, p. 186. It might also be added that Alyona was

the name of the faithful peasant nurse who brought up the Dostoyevsky children. See A.M. Dostoyevsky, 'Iz "Vospominaniy" ', *Vosp.* Vol. I, p. 42.

6. It is perhaps significant that during the ensuing conversation with Raskolnikov the reappearance of the dead in the form of ghosts is one of Svidrigaylov's main themes.

7. The full force of *perestupit'* is lost in English: the verb evokes its variant *prestupit'* 'to commit a crime' (cf. Eng. 'transgress'). The title of the novel itself, *Prestupleniye i nakazaniye,* contains this root.

8. Even this pledge proves to be in two pieces: one of metal, the other of wood (see *D.5,* p. 75).

9. Thus we are told that Porfiry has contemplated becoming a monk (though this is presented as one pole of an enigmatic nature; for on the other hand Porfiry also claims that he intends to marry) (see *D.5,* p. 267).

10. Svidrigaylo spent the eighty-odd years of his life fomenting trouble on Russia's borders. Although nominally a Roman Catholic, he allied himself with Orthodox dissidents, Hussites, and the Order of the Livonian Knights in his efforts to further his own political aims. In 1434, against the wishes of Muscovy, Svidrigaylo had Gerasim of Smolensk consecrated in Constantinople as Metropolitan of all Russia, only to have him executed the following year. The Dostoyevskys themselves were conscious of being descended from noble Lithuanian stock, and in choosing this name perhaps the author is indulging in a device typical of his writing—self-identification with his worst characters (e.g., the murderer who is the tool of the nihilists in *The Devils* is called 'Fedka the convict', and in *The Brothers Karamazov* the murderer Smerdyakov suffers from Dostoyevsky's own affliction—epilepsy).

11. Cf. D. L. Fanger. *Dostoevsky and Romantic Realism: A Study of Dostoevsky in Relation to Balzac, Dickens and Gogol,* (Harvard University Press, 1965), p. 23.

12. This idea will be taken up at length in the novel, *The Devils,* where once more it will be interwoven with the theme of heresy.

The schism [*raskol*] was a term loosely applied to all heretics within the larger Orthodox fold, although the origins of some of the more extreme sects (e.g. the Flagellants [*Khlysty*] and their offshoot the Castrates [*Skoptsy*]) appear to be largely pagan and have little, if anything, to do with the true schism in the Russian Church which took place in the seventeenth century.

Interestingly enough there was even a more recent sect which hailed

Napoleon as a new Messiah—the sect of the *Napoleonovy*. See K. K. Grass, *Die russischen Sekten,* (Leipzig, 1907), Vol. I, pp. 562–63; also P.I. Mel'nikov (Andrey Pechersky) 'Pis'ma o raskole', *Sobraniye sochineniy v shesti tomakh* (Moscow, 1963), Vol. 6, p. 238; and F. C. Conybeare, *Russian Dissenters* (Harvard University Press, 1921), p. 370.

13. This realisation is brought about, characteristically, through a certain linguistic ambivalence. The Russian *ty* = thou (cf. French 'tu') can convey both great intimacy and great contempt:

> ' "Leave me alone," Dunya implored.
>
> Svidrigaylov shuddered: this *ty* had not been pronounced as it had been formerly.
>
> "So, you do not love me?" he asked her quietly.' (*D*.5, p. 520)

14. The name Resslikh occurs in connection with her (*D*.5, p. 497) as it had in Luzhin's account of the supposed seduction by Svidrigaylov of a fourteen-year-old deaf-mute (*D*.5, p. 309). It is with this same Gertruda Karlovna Resslikh that Svidrigaylov claims to be staying, when he hires the apartment next to Sonya (*D*.5, p. 254).

15. Svidrigaylov, for example, has turned self-blame into a fine art, as a weapon to be used for the seduction of women (*D*.5, p. 497).

16. In his argument inducing Sonya to stay, Raskolnikov's final words seem charged with ironic ambiguity: ' . . . for you will remain guilty' [. . . *ved' vy zhe ostanetes' vinovaty*] (*D*.5, p. 425).

17. Dostoyevsky's distinctive use of language for each character has been remarked on. See, for example, Grossman, *Dostoyevsky*, p. 355.

A Psychologist's View

R. D. LAING

◆   ◆   ◆

The Counterpoint of Experience

DOSTOYEVSKY'S GENIUS is unmistakable in his grasp of the counterpoint of dreams, phantasy, imagination, and memory. All his novels reveal or imply simultaneous participation in these modalities. It is not easy to demonstrate this succinctly. We shall try to do so, by considering Dostoyevsky's account of Raskolnikov at the beginning of *Crime and Punishment* in terms of dream, phantasy, imagination, reality, up to and including the murder.

The modality of 'phantasy' in contrast to 'imagination' is shown clearly in Raskolnikov.

The day before he murders the old woman, Raskolnikov 'dreamed a terrible dream' (p. 72, et seq.).[1] This is a long, intricate, vivid dream. We abridge it drastically.

> ... He dreamed of the time when he was a child and when they still lived in their little provincial town. He was a boy

of seven. It was a holiday, late in the afternoon, and he was out for a walk in the country with his father.

His father and he were walking along a road to a cemetery, where were the graves of his grandmother and a brother who had died at the age of six months, whom Raskolnikov could not remember. They were passing a pub; he was holding his father's hand and gazing fearfully at the pub, which was associated with scenes of drunkenness and violence. In front of the pub there was a large cart such as would usually be pulled by a large drayhorse:

> ... but now, curiously enough, some peasant's small, lean, greyish-brown mare was harnessed to one of these huge carts, the sort of poor old nag which—he had seen it so often—found it very hard to draw quite an ordinary cart with wood or hay piled on top of it, especially when the cart was stuck in the mud or in a rut, and every time that happened, the peasant flogged her so brutally, so brutally, sometimes even across the eyes and muzzle, and he felt so sorry, so sorry for the poor old horse that he almost burst into tears, and his mother always used to take him away from the window. But now in front of the pub pandemonium suddenly broke loose: a crowd of blind drunk big peasants in red and blue shirts with their coats thrown over their shoulders came out of the pub, yelling and singing and strumming their balalaikas. 'Come on, get on my cart!' shouted one of them, quite a young peasant with a terribly thick neck and a very red, beefy face. 'I'll drive you all home! Get in!'

The poor old nag is unequal to the task imposed on her. The peasants find this a great joke:

> ... People were laughing, and indeed, how could they help laughing? The mare was all skin and bones, and there she was supposed to drag such a heavy load at a gallop! Two young lads in the cart at once took a whip each and got ready to help Mikolka.

They begin to flog her.

> 'Daddy! Daddy!' he cried to his father. 'Daddy, look what they are doing! Daddy, they're beating the poor little horse!'
>
> 'Come along, come along, son,' said his father. 'They're drunk. Having fun, the fools. Come along and don't look,' and he tried to take him away, but he tore himself out of his father's hands and hardly realizing what he was doing, ran to the old horse. But the poor old mare was already in a very bad state. She was gasping for breath, standing still, pulling at the cart again, and almost collapsing in the road.
>
> 'Flog her to death!' shouted Mikolka. 'I don't mind. I'm going to flog her to death myself!'

The joke becomes more hilarious as Mikolka's fury mounts. He shouts that she is his property.

> 'I'll damn well do what I like with her! Come on, there's plenty of room. Come on, all of you! I'm going to make her gallop if it's the last thing I do!'

Only the seven-year-old Raskolnikov feels concern for the poor old nag.

> He ran beside the old mare, he ran in front of her, he saw her being whipped across her eyes, across the very eyes! He was crying. His heart heaved. Tears rolled down his cheeks. One of the men who were flogging the horse grazed his face with the whip, but he felt nothing. Wringing his hands and screaming, he rushed up to the old man with the grey beard who was shaking his head and condemning it all. A woman took him by the hand and tried to lead him away, but he freed himself and ran back to the poor old horse, which seemed to be at the last gasp, but started kicking once more.
>
> 'Oh, to hell with you!' shouted Mikolka furiously, and, throwing down his whip, he bent down and dragged out a long thick shaft from the bottom of the cart. Taking hold of it by one end with both hands, he swung it with an effort over the grey-brown mare.

'He'll strike her dead!' they shouted all round. 'He'll kill her!'

'My property!' shouted Mikolka, and let fall the shaft with all his might. There was the sound of a heavy thud.

'Flog her! Flog her! Why have you stopped?' Shouts were heard in the crowd.

And Mikolka swung the shaft another time, and another terrific blow fell across the back of the unhappy mare. She subsided on her haunches, but presently was on her feet again, pulling, pulling with all her remaining strength first on one side and then on another, trying to move the cart. But they were belabouring her from every side with six whips, and the shaft was raised again and fell for the third and then for the fourth time, slowly and with terrific force. Mikolka was furious because he had not been able to kill her with one blow.

'Alive and kicking!' they shouted on all sides.

'Bet she'll fall down any minute now, lads,' shouted a sportsman in the crowd. 'She's about finished !'

'Why don't you strike her with an axe? Despatch her at once!' a third one shouted.

'Oh, damn her! Make way!' Mikolka yelled furiously and, throwing down the shaft, he once more bent down in the cart and pulled out an iron bar. 'Mind!' he shouted, swinging it with all his might over the poor old horse. The bar came down with a crash; the old mare swayed, subsided, and was about to give another pull at the cart when the bar once again descended on her back with terrific force, and she collapsed on the ground as though her four legs had given way from under her all at once.

'Finish her off!' Mikolka shouted, jumping down from the cart, blind with rage.

A few young men, also red-faced and drunk, seized whatever they could lay their hands on—whips, sticks, the shaft—and ran to the dying mare. Mikolka stood on one side and started raining blows across her back with the iron bar without bothering to see where the blows were falling.

The mare stretched out her head, heaved a deep sigh, and died.

'Settled her!' they shouted in the crowd.

'Why didn't she gallop?'

'My property!' shouted Mikolka, iron bar in hand and with bloodshot eyes. He stood there as though he were sorry he had nothing more to flog.

'Aye, you ain't got the fear of God in you after all,' many voices were already shouting in the crowd.

But by now the poor little boy was beside himself. He pushed his way through the crowd to the grey-brown mare, put his arms round her dead, bloodstained muzzle, and kissed her, kissed her on the eyes, on the lips. . . . Then suddenly jumped to his feet and rushed in a rage at Mikolka with his little fists. But just then his father, who had been running after him, caught hold of him at last and carried him out of the crowd.

'Come along, son, come along,' he said to him. 'Let's go home.'

'Daddy, why—why did they kill the poor little horse?' he whimpered, but suddenly his breath failed him and the words came in shrieks from his panting breast.

'They're drunk,' said his father. 'Playing the fool. It's not our business. Come along!'

He put his arms round his father, but his chest tightened and he felt choked. He tried to draw a breath, to cry out and—woke up.

Raskolnikov woke up in a cold sweat, his hair wet with perspiration, gasping for breath, and he raised himself in terror.

'Thank God it was only a dream!' he said, sitting down under a tree and drawing deep breaths. 'But what's the matter with me? These are not the symptoms of a fever, are they? What a horrid dream!'

Every bone in his body seemed to ache; his soul was in fusion and darkness. He put his elbows on his knees and propped his head on his hands.

'Good God!' he cried, 'Is it possible that I will really take a hatchet, hit her on the head with it, crack her skull, slither about in warm, sticky blood, break the lock, steal and shake with fear, hide myself all covered in blood and with the hatchet– Good God! Is it possible?'

Raskolnikov's first experience on waking shows that his own body is intimately compromised by this dream. He awoke in terror as though it was *he* who had been flogged to death, and immediately recalls with horror his intention to kill the old woman by hitting her on the head in a very similar way to the striking of the old nag.

From this, it seems that Raskolnikov's experience of his 'own' body is in terms of a physical identification with the mare and the old woman. The site of the incident is close to the cemetery wherein are the graves of his grandmother and younger brother. He does not '*imagine*' himself to be an old mare/old woman. On the contrary, 'in his imagination' he is as far as possible from the situation in which he is in his dream or in his phantasy. In his dream he is a seven-year-old boy empathizing with an old nag, while in phantasy his own body participates in the death of an old nag and old woman. But 'he', we learn later, imagines himself to be Napoleon! He is 'lost' between his imagination, where he thinks of himself as Napoleon, his dream, where he is a little boy, and his phantasy, where he is a beaten old mare and an old woman he is about to kill.

Raskolnikov is aware of his dreams and of his intention to murder the old woman money-lender. He is not aware of the link between Mikolka and the other ruthlessly violent drunken peasants and himself, or of the link between the old mare and the old woman. He does not connect the above with his 'own' feelings towards his mother. He is not aware of identifying his mother (or grandmother) with a miserly money-lender and with an old nag that is good for nothing. Nor is he aware of identifying *himself* with the old nag, his mother, or the money-lender.

When he finally 'knows' that the old woman will be murdered tomorrow, he feels himself like a man sentenced to death. In the modality of his phantasy, *he* is the victim, whereas 'in imagination' and in 'reality' he is the executioner.

Just before he enters the gates of the old woman's flat to kill her, he remarks about his own thoughts: 'It's like that, I suppose, that the thoughts of those who are led to execution cling to everything they see on the way. . . . ' That is, in phantasy he is more the victim being led to execution than the executioner.

Just before the old woman opens her door he suddenly loses the feel of his own body. It appears that in order to murder this old woman, his action-in-phantasy is to re-project 'the old nag' on to the person of the money-lender who 'in reality' means nothing to him.

Raskolnikov murders the old woman 'to be Napoleon', 'for money', or just 'for spite' as he later speculates. But Dostoyevsky discloses also his phantasy, a modality of action and experience, as a *physical dream,* in which he is submerged and contained. Thus in bondage he is estranged, with transitory moments of emergence, from participation in the 'real' world as a young man in his 'own' person. In this state, recognition of who the other is remains unavailable to him.

In this novel, the theme of the prostitute is deeply explored. The old woman is yet another *pro*-stitute, as is Raskolnikov himself, in the sense of one who stands for another. Dostoyevsky makes clear that Raskolnikov conceived a violent aversion to her 'at once, though he knew nothing about her'. The 'old woman' and her sister were experienced so much in the modality of phantasy that little else registered on Raskolnikov. Awareness that he was *phantasizing* them rather than *perceiving* them 'in their own light' was fugitive. He was trapped 'within' his phantasy. No wonder he felt stifled.

Attributions and Injunctions

We have already considered Raskolnikov in *Crime and Punishment* from the point of view of his confusion of dream, phantasy, imagination, and waking perception. Dostoyevsky not only tells us this, but relates Raskolnikov's experience to the position he is 'placed' in before the murder. He displays Raskolnikov as 'placed' in a position that could be termed 'false', 'unfeasible', 'untenable', 'impossible'.

On the day before he murders the old pawnbroker woman, *a few hours before his 'terrible dream'*, Raskolnikov receives a letter from his mother. It is a long letter, about 4,500 words.

Its length contributes some of its essential qualities. As one reads it one comes to be enveloped in an emotional fog in which it is very difficult to retain one's bearings. When this letter was read to a group of eight psychiatrists, all testified to feelings of tension in themselves; two reported that they felt physically stifled; three reported that they felt marked visceral tensions. The quality of the letter that evokes this intense response is inevitably partially lost in the following extracts, but they enable some of the 'machinery' to become apparent.

The letter begins (pp. 48 et seq.):

'My dear Roddy, . . . it is over two months now since I had a good talk with you by letter, and I was so distressed about it that it kept me awake at night, thinking. But I know you won't blame me for my unavoidable silence. You know how much I love you, dear. You are all we have in the world, Dunya and I; you are our only hope of a better and brighter future . . . '

She goes on to express concern about his career and their financial difficulties.

' . . . But now, thank God, I think I shall be able to send you a little, and as a matter of fact we can congratulate ourselves on our good fortune now, which piece of good news I make haste to share with you. But first of all, my dear Roddy, I wonder if you know that your sister has been living with me for the last six weeks and we shall never part again . . . '

We do not in fact discover what the good fortune is until about 2,000 words later, for Mrs Raskolnikov goes into a detailed ac-

count of her daughter Dunya's recent humiliation in the house
of the Svidrigaylovs. She has not told Roddy before this because

> 'If I had told you the whole truth, you would, I dare say,
> have thrown up everything and have come to us, even if
> you had to walk all the way; for I know your character and
> your feelings very well, and *I realize that you would never allow
> your sister to be humiliated.*'

Dunya's character had been besmirched by Mrs Svidrigaylov,
who had branded her as an immoral woman who was having an
affair with her husband. However, Dunya was finally publicly
vindicated, and

> '... everyone all of a sudden began to treat her with
> marked respect. All this was the chief reason for the quite
> unexpected turn of events, which I may say has completely
> changed our prospects. For I must tell you now, dear
> Roddy, that Dunya has received an offer of marriage, and
> that she has already given her consent, of which I now
> hasten to inform you. And though all this has been ar-
> ranged without your advice, I am sure you will not be cross
> with me or your sister, for I hope you will agree that it was
> quite impossible for us to postpone Dunya's answer till we
> received a reply from you. And, besides, I don't expect you
> could have made up your mind without being present here
> yourself. It all happened like this ... '

There follows a description of Dunya's fiancé, Peter Luzhin, 'a
civil servant with the rank of a counsellor', which is a masterpiece
of its kind.

> ' ... He is a distant relative of Mrs Svidrigaylov's, and it was
> indeed she who was chiefly instrumental in arranging the
> match.... He had coffee with us, and the very next day we
> received a letter from him in which he very courteously
> asked for Dunya's hand in marriage and begged for a defi-
> nite and speedy answer. He is a practical man and very busy,
> and he is now in a hurry to leave for Petersburg, so that

every minute is precious to him. We were naturally very much surprised at first, for all this had happened very quickly and unexpectedly. We spent the whole of that day discussing the matter, wondering what was the best thing to do. He is a very safe and reliable man, has two official jobs, and already has money of his own. It is true he is forty-five years old, but he is fairly good-looking, and I dare say women might still find him attractive. He is altogether a highly respectable and dignified man, though perhaps a little morose and overbearing. But quite possibly that is only the first impression he makes on people. And, please, Roddy dear, I must ask you not to judge him too hastily and too heatedly when you meet him in Petersburg, which will probably be very soon, as I'm afraid you're all too likely to do if something about him does not appeal to you at the first glance. I'm saying this, dear, just in case, for I'm quite sure that he will make a good impression on you. And, besides, to get to know any man properly one must do it gradually and carefully so as to avoid making a mistake and becoming prejudiced, for such mistakes and prejudices are very difficult to overcome and put right afterwards. Mr Luzhin, to judge by many signs, is a highly worthy gentleman. . . . There is of course no special love either on her side or on his, but Dunya is a clever girl and as noble-minded as an angel, and she will consider it her duty to make her husband happy, and he, too, will probably do his best to make her happy, at least we have no good reason to doubt it, though I must say the whole thing has happened rather in a hurry. Besides he is a very shrewd man, and he will of course realize that the happier be makes Dunya, the happier his own married life will be. As for a certain unevenness in his character, certain odd habits, and even certain differences of opinion (which can hardly be avoided in the happiest marriages) Dunya has told herself that there is nothing to worry about. . . . He struck me at first . . . as rather harsh, but after all, that is probably because he is such an outspoken man, and indeed I am sure that is why.'

The next section of the letter is dedicated mainly to conveying the idea that the only possible reason that Dunya is marrying this obviously insufferably smug bore and tyrant is for Roddy's sake.

'... Dunya and I have already decided that even now you could start on your career and regard your future as absolutely settled. Oh, if only that were so! This would be of so great an advantage to you that we must regard it as nothing less than a special sign of God's grace to us, *Dunya can think of nothing else.*'

Later:

'... Dunya is thinking of nothing else now. During the last few days she seems to have been in a kind of fever, and she has already formed a whole plan about your becoming Mr Luzhin's assistant later, and even a partner in his legal business, particularly as you are studying law yourself.'

Finally, she tells him that she and Dunya are coming to St Petersburg for Dunya's marriage, which 'for certain private reasons of his own' Luzhin wishes to get over as soon as possible.

'... Oh, how happy I shall be to press you to my heart! Dunya is terribly excited and happy to be able to see you so soon, and she even told me once, as a joke, of course, that she'd gladly have married Luzhin for that alone. She is an angel!'

The letter ends:

'... And now, Roddy, my precious darling, let me embrace you till we meet again. Bless you, my darling! Love Dunya, Roddy. Love your sister. Love her as much as she loves you, and remember she loves you very much, much more than herself. She is an angel, and you, Roddy, are all we have in the world, our only hope of a better and brighter future. If only you are happy we shall be happy. Do you still say your prayers, Roddy, as you used to, and do you believe in the goodness and mercy of our Creator and our Redeemer? I am, in my heart, afraid that you may have succumbed to the influence of the modern spirit of godlessness. If so, then I pray for you. Remember, dear, how as a child, while your father was still with us, you used to lisp your prayers on my knees and how happy we all were then? Goodbye, or rather *au revoir.* Let me hold you close to me, my darling, and kiss you again and again.

Yours to the grave,
Pulcheria Raskolnikov'

Raskolnikov's immediate response to the letter is as follows:

Almost all the time he was reading the letter, from the very beginning, Raskolnikov's face was wet with tears; but when he had finished it, his face was pale and contorted, and a bitter, spiteful, evil smile played on his lips. He put his head on his old pillow and thought a long, long time. His heart was beating fast and his thoughts were in a whirl. At last he felt stifled and cramped in that yellow cubby-hole of his, which was more like a cupboard or a box than a room. His eyes and his thoughts craved for more space. He grabbed his hat and went out, without worrying this time whether he met anyone on the stairs or not; he forgot all about it. He walked in the direction of Vassilyevsky Island along Voznessensky Avenue, as though he were in a hurry to get there on some business, but, as usual, he walked without noticing where he was going, muttering and even talking aloud to himself, to the astonishment of the passers-by, many of whom thought he was drunk.

Let us consider the position that Raskolnikov is placed in by this letter. He is told: 'I realize that you would never allow your sister to be humiliated.' He is also told that his sister, after one frightfully humiliating experience, is in the process of undergoing what, as his mother makes clear to him, is an even greater humiliation. Whereas in the first instance she herself was blameless, in the second instance, by entering into a marriage that is no more than legalized prostitution, she is corrupting her own integrity. He is told that she is doing this only for his sake. And this he is expected to welcome.

But he has already been defined by his mother as a man who would never allow his sister to be humiliated. Is he at the same time to be a man who will allow her to sell herself for his sake? This is an untenable position.

Another twist to the tourniquet is turned around happiness. 'If only you are happy, we shall be happy.' In terms of the person he is supposed to be, how could he be made happy by such a state of affairs?

Yet another turn is added in respect of religion and godlessness. The whole concern of the major part of the letter is the sacrifice of one person's life, in order to provide enough money for another to get on in the world. This is taken as an index of Dunya's 'heart of gold', a suitably ambiguous expression, and of what an angel she is.

However, what is the position of a Christian placed in the position of being the recipient of this gratuity?

Dunya and her mother are only too glad to sacrifice themselves to invest in Roddy, 'our only hope for a better and brighter future'. On the one hand, they evidently wish him to make money in order to get them out of their rut. On the other hand, they tell him that all they want from him is his 'happiness'. Simultaneously, his mother fears that he may have succumbed to the 'modern spirit of godlessness' such as putting 'the world' before love!

To tease out all the strands in the entanglements of this letter, or even in the above extracts, the unavowed contradictions and paradoxes, the multi-levels of hypocrisy, would require an examination many times longer than the letter itself.

In reading the letter it is a useful exercise to imagine what would be the likely effect on the person for whom it is meant. As pointed out above, we must think transpersonally, not simply of the disturbance *in* the letter, but its disturb*ing* impact on another.

To summarize some aspects.

The person to whom it is addressed is placed in a non-compossible set of positions all at once.

There is a pervasive implicit injunction to collude at each of the multi-levels of hypocrisy; other attributions imply the impossibility of the addressee doing so; others in effect forbid him to be hypocritical, especially the final reference to the unspoiled religion of childhood, when the words are really believed for what they are.

He ought to be happy, because then 'we shall be happy'. But being the man his mother tells him he is, he could never be so at his sister's great 'sacrifice'. Yet if he is not happy, he is making them unhappy. So presumably he will be selfish if he is happy, and selfish if he is unhappy and guilty to be happy, and guilty to be unhappy.

Dunya is repeatedly defined as an angel. 'Look what she is prepared to do for you', in effect. This carries an implicit negative injunction against daring to define her in a negative way, at the expense of being ungrateful. He would have to be a monster to have any feelings other than gratitude to such a heavenly creature, whose heart is eighteen carat, or to construe her action as any other than self-sacrifice. Yet if he is the man he is told he is, he must prevent it. Unless he does something awful, it is already *almost* a *fait accompli.* While being given grounds for hatred, resentment, bitterness, shame, guilt, humiliation, impotence, at the same time he is told that he should be happy. To move in any direction sanctioned by the letter, or to sustain consistently one position among the numerous incompatibilities *in* the letter, requires him to be defined within the framework of the letter as spiteful and evil.

He must not judge Luzhin too hastily or too heatedly when he meets him, 'as I'm afraid you're all too likely to do if something about him does not appeal to you at the first glance', although 'I'm quite sure that he will make a good impression on you.' The letter then proceeds to make it impossible that Luzhin could make anything but the worst possible impression on him.

He ought to be a Christian. But if he is a Christian, he would be evil to endorse such a godless plan for gaining money and social status in the world. He could endorse this plan if he were godless, but if he were godless he would be evil.

His thoughts in a whirl, stifled by the obligation to be grateful for this unsolicited sacrifice, he goes out, ruminating on how to stop Dunya marrying this awful man. Through their actions, his future is decided, unless he does something terrible, and this future is impossible.

The letter as it were explodes inside him. He is shattered, as one says. Dostoyevsky gives us some of the debris. Napoleon in imagination, a little boy in his dream, an old nag-woman in phantasy, a murderer in fact. Finally, through his crime and punishment, he wins through to Sonia, and Dunya finds happiness with his friend Razumihkin. His mother dies mad.

Notes

1. Page references are to F. Dostoyevsky, *Crime and Punishment*, Harmondsworth, Penguin Books, 1951.

Crime and Punishment and Contemporary Radical Thought

DEREK OFFORD

❖ ❖ ❖

I

D OSTOYEVSKY, WHEN HE CAME to write *Crime and Punishment* in 1865, had already made an extensive contribution, both in publicism and in imaginative literature, to the vigorous intellectual life of those years following the Crimean War and the death of Nicholas I when a more liberal regime flowered briefly in Russia and when the old order began to undergo irreversible change. In particular the hostility towards the radical camp which found expression in Dostoyevsky's writing in the early sixties was to become one of the prime creative influences in his major fiction.[1]

The radical camp, of course, contained individuals with divergent opinions. Moreover, the Western thinkers from whom the Russian radicals derived their convictions were themselves numerous and of varied complexion, ranging from the English utilitarian Jeremy Bentham, the early Welsh socialist Robert Owen, French utopian socialists such as Fourier, Cabet and Considerant, and the positivist Comte, to German philosophers and thinkers such as Feuerbach and L. Büchner, the contemporary English historian Buckle, scientists such as Darwin and popularizers of scientific thought, such as G. H. Lewes. But it is probably not grossly inaccurate to suggest that what was of most interest in Western thought to the Russian radicals of the sixties, and what constituted for Dostoyevsky a core against which his creative energies should be directed, might be reduced to a fairly limited number of propositions which were given wide currency in the journal *Contemporary* and in the voluminous, wordy and extremely influential writings of Chernyshevsky in particular.

These propositions may be summarized as follows: firstly, that 'no dualism is to be seen in man',[2] that is to say man does not possess a spiritual dimension which is qualitatively different from his physical being; secondly, that man is governed by self-interest; thirdly, that he is at the same time a rational creature; fourthly, that he may therefore be made to see where his best interest lies and to act accordingly; fifthly, that since man is amenable to rational persuasion and since his best interest lies in cooperation with his fellows, one might realistically hope to construct in theory and then in practice a perfectly ordered society; sixthly, that the good is that which is useful, and the useful, for the radical 'men of the sixties', was in turn that which promoted the dissemination and acceptance of the preceding propositions; and finally, that a scientific method of enquiry, and only that method of enquiry (with the help of which all the preceding propositions were supposedly formulated), could be applied successfully and profitably to the examination of human conduct, society and government.

Dostoyevsky disagrees profoundly with every one of these propositions. In his first major novel, *Crime and Punishment,* he makes explicit or oblique references, which are caustic in their context, to thinkers who defend them,[3] and vigorously disputes the propositions themselves. He implies, for example, that it is resurrection of the spiritual side of Raskolnikov's being which offers him his only hope of salvation after he has taken other lives. Furthermore, it is love of others, as preached and practised by Sonya, rather than love of self, which makes possible such regeneration. Raskolnikov is not capable of consistently rational conduct. His behaviour is frequently self-destructive. And Razumikhin inveighs bitterly against the socialist utopia (VI, 197; III, v). But in particular Dostoyevsky sets out to test in his novel the strength and acceptability of the last two propositions of the radicals, which concern the equation of the good with the useful and the omnicompetence of the scientific method of enquiry.[4] And it is through his examination of the subjects of the causes of crime and the nature and status of law that Dostoyevsky explores the implications of these two propositions and concentrates his argument against those who defend them.

II

There are no doubt several reasons for Dostoyevsky's choice of the subjects of crime and the law as his ground on which to do battle with the radicals.

Firstly, legal questions very much preoccupied educated people in Russia in the early 1860s, and the novelist of the time, with his interest in contemporary reality, was entitled to devote attention to them. Overhaul of the judicial system was one aspect of the great reforms planned and carried out in Russia in the late 1850s and early 60s. An ukase of 1864 finally provided for the establishment of new courts on the Western model. Numerous foreign books on jurisprudence were translated, published and reviewed in this period and the journals devoted much attention to legal questions. Dostoyevsky's own journal *Epoch,* for example carried lengthy articles on legal procedure, punishments, criminal law and lawyers, as well as the memoirs of an investigator, in the course of 1864–65.[5] In 1865 Dostoyevsky himself was contemplating an article on the courts, some notes for which are preserved in one of his notebooks.[6] Thus references to changes in the law and its administration, the proliferation of the legal profession, litigation, the increase in crime—there are allusions to forgery, seduction, and poisoning, as well as description of Raskolnikov's murders, in *Crime and Punishment*—help on one level to provide a broad social backcloth for the novel's main action.

Secondly, on a deeper level, the mentality of the criminal was a subject that already absorbed Dostoyevsky, the novelist of profound psychological insight. He had intimate knowledge of the criminal, gained in his years in prison among hardened convicts and recorded in *Notes from the House of the Dead.* In the journal *Time,* which he had edited from 1861 to 1863, there had appeared transcripts of famous trials of the century, and Dostoyevsky himself had written a preface to the first transcript (XIX, 89–90), dealing with the trial of the French professional criminal Lacenaire, a murderer who exhibits striking similarities to Raskolnikov (both Lacenaire and Raskolnikov are educated but impoverished young men driven obsessively to dominate; both are influenced by Napoleon, atheistic, antisocial and vengeful; and both publish speculative articles, Raskolnikov on crime and Lacenaire on the penal system).[7] It may also be that the great fictional possibilities of the subject of crime and its detection were underlined for Dostoyevsky by the novels of Dickens, in so many of which crime, including murder, is a central feature.

Thirdly, on the polemical level, the question of crime was one which also preoccupied the socialists with whom Dostoyevsky was taking issue. Like their Western European mentors, the Russian radicals of the 1860s expressed deterministic views on the causes of crime which seemed to Dostoyevsky as oversimplified as their views on the nature of man and his society. Robert Owen—whom Chernyshevsky's hero, Lopukhov, describes as a 'holy old man' and whose portrait hangs in Lopukhov's room—had taught the Russian radicals that crime was a natural product of the irrational organization of the British society of his day.[8] The 'poor and uneducated profligate among the working classes', he wrote in his *New View of Society,* 'are now trained to commit crimes'; but with man's natural progression from a 'state of ignorance to intelligence', and the consequent implementation of 'rational plans for the education and general formation' of a society's members, crime would be eradicated. 'Withdraw these circumstances which tend to create crime in the human character', he wrote with the ingenuous benevolence of the early socialists, 'and crime will not be created', for the 'worst formed disposition, short of incurable insanity', would not long resist a 'firm, determined, well-directed, persevering kindness'.[9] Similarly, Büchner, who in the late fifties and early sixties exercised an influence on the Russian radical intelligentsia out of all proportion to his importance in the history of European thought, argued in *Kraft und Stoff*—a work much admired, incidentally, by Bazarov—that the 'chief causes of crime' were deficiency of intellect, poverty and want of education'.[10] In the Russia of the 1860s, where it became customary to explain a man's behaviour deterministically, as a product of his environment, views such as these were commonplace. Chernyshevsky, for example, in his major profession of faith, the article on the 'anthropological principle in philosophy', asserted:

'After the need to breathe . . . man's most pressing need is to eat and drink. Very often, very many people lack the wherewithal for the proper satisfaction of this need, and this lack is the source of the greatest number of all bad actions, of almost all situations and institutions which are constant causes of bad actions. If one were to remove this cause of evil alone, at least nine tenths of all that is bad would quickly disappear from human society: the number of crimes would decrease ten times.'[11]

Likewise Dobrolyubov stated, in the tortuous style characteristic of the radical publicism of the time, that 'any crime is not a consequence of man's nature, but a consequence of the abnormal relationship to society in which he is placed'.[12] Dostoyevsky's antagonism to such views is a major source of tension in *Crime and Punishment*.

III

Now it is one of the qualities of Dostoyevsky as a novelist that he seems rarely to come down decisively in his works of art on the side of those views which it is clear from his publicistic works that he wished to promote. His vision as an artist is too complex to permit him to be one-sided or tendentious. It is arguable, for example, that he failed adequately to rebut the arguments of Ivan Karamazov against acceptance of God's world, although he himself evidently needed to disbelieve them. And by emphasizing the loathsomeness of the pawnbroker Alyona and the exploitative Luzhin he sets up persuasive arguments in *Crime and Punishment* in favour of the crime whose moral inadmissibility he undoubtedly hoped eventually to demonstrate.

Similarly he does not simply reject out of hand the radicals' thesis that poverty was a possible cause of crime (or at least a cause of the derangement which might induce it). On the contrary, he points out on the very first page of the novel that Raskolnikov was 'crushed by poverty' (VI, 5; I, i); for the second day running, we read shortly afterwards, he had eaten virtually nothing (VI, 6; I, i), and clearly his debility and illness are related. The oppressive and stinking milieu, moreover, 'jarred the young man's nerves which were already disturbed without that' (VI, 6; I, i). And when Raskolnikov does refresh himself after his first visit to Alyona's, his thoughts clear and all that has been passing through his mind suddenly seems nonsense, the result of physical disorder (VI, 10–11; I, i). Furthermore, the view that crime and social conditions are related is openly advanced in those chapters of the novel in which characters, with the murder of Alyona and Lizaveta in mind, debate the causes of crime. Luzhin, trying to restore his rapidly dwindling credit when he visits Raskolnikov in part II, delivers himself of a disquisition on the growth of crime in Russia, a phenomenon which Zosimov attributes to the fact that there have been 'many economic changes' (VI, 118; II, v). Later, during Raskolnikov's first visit to Porfiry, Razumikhin refers to a heated debate that had taken place the night before, in which someone had expressed the view of the 'socialists' that 'crime is a protest against the abnormality of the social order—and only that, and nothing more, and no other causes are admitted'. According to this view 'all crimes' would disappear once society was organized 'normally' (VI, 196 III, v). It is a view which even Porfiry appears to endorse: ' "environment" means a lot in crime', he affirms. And he seems prepared to carry it to the extreme, since when Razumikhin asks him whether 'environment' could be said to explain the seduction of a ten-year-old girl by a forty-year-old man, he replies 'with surprising gravity': 'Well, in a strict sense it very probably is environment, even a crime committed against a little girl may very well be explained by "environment" ' (VI, 197; III, v). Lebezyatnikov argues with even more conviction in favour of such social determinism. He believes that everything depends on man's 'surroundings' and 'environment'. 'All on the environment', he says in his broken Russian, 'and man himself is nothing' (VI, 283; V, i). In the society of the future, therefore, when all is rationally arranged in the interests of equality, there will not even be any fights (VI, 281–2; V, i).

However, we are not expected to accept the deterministic view of man's behaviour and of the incidence of crime uncritically. We are put on our guard against it by the fact that its advocates are, in Dostoyevsky's terms, unreliable. Zosimov, for example, merely voices the commonplaces fashionable among the younger generation. As a doctor he is the novel's main practitioner of the exact sciences which that generation exalted. He is the target of the invective of Razumikhin—the physically and spiritually healthy foil to the sickly Raskolnikov—against the 'dumb progressives' who understand nothing and show disrespect for man because they take too narrow a view of him (VI, 104; II, iv). And in practice Zosimov's judgement is repeatedly at fault: for instance he mistakenly assumes the murderer to be an experienced criminal (VI, 117; II, v); he wrongly predicts that the arrival of Raskolnikov's mother and sister will have a beneficial effect on Raskolnikov (VI, 159; III, i); and he fails to see in what way Luzhin is a bad suitor for Dunya (VI, 163; III, ii). As for Lebezyatnikov, he is discredited morally—he beats Katerina Marmeladova (VI, 14; I, ii)—and intellectually—he is the main apostle of Western rationalism in the novel but has great difficulty in talking coherently in his native language (VI, 307; V, iii). And Porfiry, although he is by no means an object of Dostoyevsky's criticism, does have a notorious capacity to mislead others for his own ends (VI, 197–8; III, v). On the other hand Razumikhin, the most vehement opponent of the view that 'crime is a protest against the abnormality of the social order' and 'nothing more' (VI, 196; III, v), is the champion of values close to Dostoyevsky's own. Indeed in a sense he is the 'positive hero' of the novel, Dostoyevsky's fictional response to the hero of Chernyshevsky's *What Is To Be Done?* Rakhmetov, with whom Dostoyevsky even confuses him at one point in a rough draft for one of the scenes of *Crime and Punishment*.[13] Like Rakhmetov, Razumikhin is physically strong, resourceful, independent, strong-willed and solicitous for his friends. He too is capable of feats of great endurance: Rakhmetov lies on a bed of nails to strengthen his will;[14] Razumikhin has gone through a whole winter without heating his room (VI, 44; I, iv).

More importantly, besides casting doubt on the reliability of those who uphold the deterministic explanation of crime or appear to do so, Dostoyevsky underlines the limitations of the explanation itself by demonstrating—as was habitual with him— that the problem could be approached from the opposite angle. The radicals' hatred of existing society and their overriding desire to bring about its material transformation lead them to attribute even individual acts of wrongdoing to unsatisfactory social conditions.[15] Dostoyevsky, on the other hand, being concerned above all with the spiritual condition of the individual, seeks to direct the attention of those who would examine the incidence of crime in a given society not so much to any aspects of the material environment as to those psychological factors which allow the individual to commit crime or fail to prevent him from doing so. Thus in *Crime and Punishment* he is perhaps less interested in motives for murder, such as the desire of the impoverished Raskolnikov to 'get rich quick' (VI, 27; I, iii), than in the modern attitudes which appear to make it irrational for him not to kill, given the weakening or absence of conscience. In particular he has in mind the utilitarian morality of the radicals who, in the course of their endeavours to redefine concepts and transform values associated with the established order, described the good as that which was useful and the greatest good as that which was useful to the greatest number, and commended the moral doctrine which they designated 'rational egoism'.

As critics have frequently pointed out, Dostoyevsky emphasizes the prevalence of the utilitarian morality of the radicals and makes clear its bearing on the murder which Raskolnikov commits.[16] In the letter to his prospective publisher Katkov, which he drafted in September 1865 when *Crime and Punishment* was taking shape in his mind, Dostoyevsky associated his hero's crime with current theories: the action was to take place in that year and the hero, who was to be a 'man of the new generation', had been carried away by certain badly thought out ideas which were 'in the air'.[17] Moreover, in order to emphasize that conversations about the possibility of killing in the interests of public utility were commonplace among the young generation, Dostoyevsky has Raskolnikov overhear a student advancing '*exactly the same ideas*' as those he himself is pondering (VI, 55; I, vi). (It is significant too that these ideas are put forward by a student, for it was in the higher educational institutions that the radicals found their most enthusiastic support.) Again, Porfiry emphasizes that the murder of the pawnbroker is a 'modern' crime and that the murderer killed 'in accordance with theory' (VI, 348; VI, ii).

But how precisely does the ascendancy of the new morality account for the commission of crimes which the proponents of that morality would attribute to social deprivation? The morality of the radicals, Dostoyevsky seems to argue, may produce such destructive results in three ways. Firstly, the adoption of utility as the criterion by which to judge the value of actions makes for a blurring of distinctions between acts which are absolutely right and acts which are absolutely wrong, that is right or wrong, moral or immoral, in all circumstances. Judgement of the quality of an action becomes dependent on extrinsic factors such as the value of its probable consequences. Seen from this point of view, acts which have traditionally appeared to be immoral are no longer necessarily held to be so. Lebezyatnikov exhibits this relativistic attitude when he says that what in the present society is 'stupid' may in the rationally ordered society of the future be 'intelligent' (VI, 283; V, i). But more importantly Raskolnikov himself applies it to crime. The murder, when its advantages have been calculated and the sum of its disadvantages subtracted, seems a useful act and is therefore " 'not a crime' " (VI, 59; I, vi).

Secondly, by asserting the pre-eminence of the greatest number, utilitarianism tends to reduce individual human beings to mere ciphers who have value not so much in themselves as in relation to the larger groups to which they belong. It was not difficult to decide, Chernyshevsky wrote, on whose side 'theoretical justice' lay: the interests of mankind in general stood higher than the advantage of an individual nation, the general interest of a whole nation stood higher than the advantage of a single class, and the interest of a numerous class stood higher than that of a numerically inconsiderable group. This 'theoretical justice' had about it an inflexible quality which precluded appeal by the minorities or individuals who might be the victims of its implementation; it represented merely an 'application of geometrical axioms' such as the " 'whole is greater than part of it' ".[18] Likewise for Dostoyevsky's student in part I of *Crime and Punishment* 'justice' (VI, 55; I, vi) consists in the promotion of the interests of the many at the expense of the pawnbroker and may be expressed simply and indisputably in the form of an equation: 'What do you think, wouldn't one tiny little crime be cancelled out by thousands of good deeds? For one life—thousands of lives, saved from rotting and decay. One death and a hundred lives in exchange—why it's arithmetic, isn't it?' (VI, 54; I, vi).[19]

Thirdly, by their doctrine of 'rational egoism'—in which the Russian utilitarianism of the 1860s chiefly found expression—the radicals tended to vindicate *egoistic* actions if the consequences of those actions could be claimed to have general utility. In this doctrine—which appears oddly incompatible with the socialist convictions it was supposed to bolster—the radicals contrived to accommodate both the proposition that man was governed by self-interest and belief in the feasibility of a utopia based on co-operation, by maintaining that man, when properly enlightened, would derive his selfish pleasure from performing acts of general utility. Raskolnikov clearly finds justification for his crime in the doctrine's identification of pursuit of personal profit, on the one hand, and promotion of general well-being, on the other (even though later, when he hears Luzhin parrot the doctrine (VI, 116; IL v), he is repelled by this potentiality in it (VI, 118; II, v)). For Raskolnikov seems to believe, as it was Dostoyevsky's intention that he should, that the murder of the pawnbroker and the theft of her money would benefit both himself and others: it would alleviate his own poverty but would also liberate his exploited sister from Luzhin and rid society of a louse.

Thus the radicals, far from providing a correct explanation of the incidence of crime in society, are putting forward moral views which are themselves responsible for crime's growth. The establishment of their doctrines, whose apparently incontestable veracity seemed to Chernyshevsky to preclude any 'unsteadiness in convictions',[20] has, in the view of Dostoyevsky and those who were likeminded, had the opposite effect: it has actually produced a discernible 'unsteadiness in the moral order'.[21] And far from tending to hasten the advent of a utopia in which acts hitherto considered criminal cease to be perpetrated, these doctrines encourage the development of an anarchic society in which such acts merely cease to be considered criminal and therefore may proliferate.

IV

From the early stages of *Crime and Punishment* Dostoyevsky puts forward implicit arguments against the acceptability and even against the practicability of the utilitarian rationalization of crime. In the first place Raskolnikov himself tends to criticize rationalistic thinking when those he loves are the victims of its application. He is infuriated, for example, at the prospect of statisticians treating his sister as merely a number in a table indicating the percentage of the population which turns to prostitution each year (I, 43; I, iv). In the second place, there are strong indications that human behaviour is not so exclusively rational as the utilitarians believe: Raskolnikov's crime is logically planned—he even measures the distance, ('exactly 730' paces (VI, 7; I, i)) between his lodging and the pawnbroker's—

and yet over its actual commission his reason has very little control. (Indeed he is forced to commit another murder, the need for which he had planned to obviate by ensuring that Lizaveta would not be at home.) Moreover, the deliberate artistic confusion of the first part of the novel, with its disjointed time sequence and sometimes fractured style, serves to point up the disorientation of the character to whom issues seem in theory to be so clear-cut. But although these factors serve from the beginning to undermine the value of the morality Raskolnikov has adopted, in fact the search for a sound explanation of his crime leads deeper into error. For the theories which Dostoyevsky has Raskolnikov express in part III of the novel, concerning the right of certain individuals to 'cross over' normal moral boundaries and to commit acts generally deemed criminal, represent an examination of some of the further implications of the new outlook. Whereas the first apparent explanation of the murder raises the question of how an act should be judged and affirms that its utility should be calculated, the second explanation raises the question as to who should make that judgement and calculation.

Commentators have drawn attention to the relationship between, on the one hand, the ideas Raskolnikov expresses in part III of the novel, and, on the other, those advanced in a book by Napoleon III and in the works of certain Russian radicals who wrote for the journal *Russian Word* and were by 1865 conducting an acrimonious polemic with the epigones of Chernyshevsky on *Contemporary*.[22] It has also been noted that the use of the word *raskol,* chosen by Dostoyevsky to denote the schism in the radical intelligentsia in the title of an article published in 1864 in his journal *Epoch*[23] (which on more than one occasion mentioned the disagreements among the radicals with evident satisfaction),[24] would seem to anticipate the name, Raskolnikov, chosen by him for the hero of the novel he began to write in the following year.[25] And, of course, Lebezyatnikov refers obliquely to this schism in the novel itself (VI, 283; V, i). But since a few very striking similarities between the views expressed in *Russian Word* and those of Raskolnikov have not been fully brought out, it is worth briefly glancing again at this polemic and at the writings of Pisarev in particular.

In many respects Pisarev's views coincide with Chernyshevsky's. Pisarev preaches a materialistic doctrine similar to Chernyshevsky's; he believes that man is governed by self-interest; he repeatedly upholds the view that it is profitable for the individual to behave in socially useful ways; and he writes an extended encomium to the new men who practise this doctrine and whom Chernyshevsky had portrayed in his novel *What Is To Be Done?*[26] But Pisarev's rebellion is altogether more iconoclastic than Chernyshevsky's. Whereas Chernyshevsky, writing in 1855 as the old order was just beginning to weaken, had given the cautious title *Aesthetic Relations of Art to Reality* to the dissertation in which he called in question the old belief that the beautiful was superior to everyday reality,[27] Pisarev, writing in 1865, when the attack on the old order was well advanced, undertook nothing less than a 'destruction' *(razrusheniye)* of aesthetics.[28] Old barriers were to be torn down unceremoniously. Literature, Pisarev wrote in 1861, for example, should strive to emancipate man 'from the various constraints imposed on him by the timidity of his own thought, by caste prejudices, by the authority of tradition, by the striving towards a common ideal and by all the obsolete lumber that prevents a living man from breathing freely and developing in every direction'.[29] His readers were exhorted to try to 'live a full life', without stifling what was *original* in them in order to accommodate the established order and the taste of the crowd. He urged the destruction, together with other old values, of that 'artificial system of morality' which crushed people from the cradle.[30] In short, Pisarev's doctrines are partially similar to those of Chernyshevsky; but, as Dostoyevsky jotted in his notebooks, probably under the impression of the article from which I have quoted, 'Pisarev has gone further'.[31] In *Crime and Punishment* Lebezyatnikov, claiming that he would argue even with Dobrolyubov were he to rise from his grave, makes the same point in similar terms. 'We have gone further in our convictions', he says, identifying himself with Pisarev and his supporters. 'We reject more' (VI, 283; V, i).

Now it very often happened that ideas being expressed in the Russian publicism of the age were embodied in the fiction and that the fiction in turn stimulated the publicism. In fact between the publicism and the fiction there existed an intimate relationship; they responded to one another and moved forward together dialectically. And the freedom from traditional restraints already being advocated by Pisarev in 1861 found its fictional representation in Bazarov, the literary prototype of the new man to whom Turgenev applied the title 'nihilist'. Pisarev was delighted to accept Bazarov as an example for the new generation to follow, although in the second of the two substantial tracts he devoted to examination of Turgenev's novel he preferred the name 'realist'.[32] The mission of the new man, as Bazarov saw it, was not to build but to destroy what impeded new construction, 'to clear space',[33] and Pisarev gleefully proceeded to elaborate on the freedom the destroyer would enjoy. Armed with an extreme materialism that obliged him to acknowledge only what his five senses could apprehend, and governed only by personal whim and self-interest, Bazarov acted 'everywhere and in everything' only as he wished or as seemed to him 'profitable and convenient'. 'Neither over himself, nor outside himself, nor within himself does he acknowledge any regulator, any moral law, any principle'.[34] That such freedom might be a basis for anarchy Pisarev plainly foresaw, since he considered it necessary to answer the question as to why Bazarov does not turn to crime. But his answer was unconvincing. Only circumstances and personal taste, he wrote, make such men as Bazarov 'honest' or 'dishonest', 'civic dignitaries or inveterate swindlers'. Nothing but personal taste, he continued in terms strikingly pertinent to *Crime and Punishment,* 'prevents them from killing and robbing' and nothing but personal taste 'prompts people of this stamp to make discoveries in the field of science and public life'. Pisarev did invoke rational egoism as a restraining factor: intelligent people realize that 'it is very profitable to be honest and that any crime, starting with a simple lie and ending with homicide, is dangerous and, consequently. inconvenient'.[35] But the die was cast. Pisarev, as Masaryk has put it, had 'vindicated for the nihilists the right to kill and to rob'.[36]

Those who are capable of exercising the new moral freedom possess great power, as Turgenev, Pisarev and Dostoyevsky all realized.[37] They enjoy an implicit superiority over those who remain bound by conventional restraints. In his essay on Bazarov, Pisarev underlined this division of humanity. On the one hand he saw the mass, whose members never use their brains independently. The mass 'neither makes discoveries, nor commits crimes'; it lives quietly from day to day 'according to the established norm'. On the other hand he saw the intelligent individuals who cannot come to terms so easily with all that the mass accepts. These individuals fall into three categories. Firstly, there are those who, being uneducated, are unable properly to take themselves in hand when they withdraw from the herd. Secondly, there are those who are educated but incapable of carrying their rebellion beyond a theoretical stage. And thirdly, there are those who are capable of implementing in practice their theoretical rebellion. These 'people of the third category' *(tret'yego razryada)* 'acknowledge their dissimilarity to the mass and boldly mark themselves off from it by their acts, by their habits, by their whole way of life . . . Here the individual attains his full self-liberation, his full individuality and independence'.[38] Chernyshevsky, at the end of his publicistic career, draws a somewhat similar distinction in *What Is To Be Done?* between 'ordinary people'[39] and those who are by implication extraordinary, although now the rational egoists Lopukhov and Kirsanov (who, as their names imply, have grown symbolically out of Turgenev's representatives of the young generation)[40] are themselves only ordinary before the epitome of independence, the iron-willed 'special man' Rakhmetov.[41]

Now Raskolnikov's speculative article on crime which is discussed in part III of *Crime and Punishment* owes much to current views such as Pisarev's on the division of mankind into the enslaved and the liberated. Indeed Raskolnikov says that what he is describing 'has been printed and read a thousand times' (VI, 200; III, v). Like Pisarev, as Dostoyevsky saw him, Raskolnikov has not merely flirted with rational egoism but has 'gone further'. He aspires, like Bazarov, to membership of that category of people who are bound by no moral law and who may waive those moral considerations that have generally restrained men from committing antisocial acts and continue to prevent the masses from doing so. Thus Raskolnikov has granted himself licence to destroy human life. He has committed the murder and robbery which Pisarev's destroyers might contemplate and has pondered the scientific discoveries and contributions to society which they might make if 'personal taste' disposed them to such actions. And he has murdered, it now appears, for no sound financial reason, but merely to confirm the freedom Pisarev had exalted. He is one of those who might be able to say a '*new word*' (VI, 200; III, v), the original contribution which Pisarev urged his readers not to stifle. His terms of reference are those of Pisarev too, although he has carried out a further simplification: the first category *(pervyy razryad)* is the mass, conservative by nature, which lives obediently; the second category *(vtoroy razryad)* consists of the 'extraordinary' men and women, the 'people of the future', the 'destroyers' *(razrushiteli)* (VI, 200; III, v). Finally, the elitism implicit in Pisarev's schema is reflected in Raskolnikov's pride, his arrogance towards 'ordinary' mortals. It is a trait which Dostoyevsky is concerned to underline at this particular point in the novel. Thus in the notes for part III he remarks that the 'thought of immeasurable pride, arrogance, and contempt for society' are expressed in Raskolnikov's personality;[42] and in the finished work Razumikhin tells Raskolnikov's mother and sister that his friend is 'arrogant and proud' (VI, 165; III, ii).

Raskolnikov, then, represents Dostoyevsky's conception of the man moulded by the new outlook and once all inhibitions have been properly stripped away. The self-will of this man accounts for a number of other traits in Raskolnikov's character which are brought out in the novel together with the explanation of the murder of Alyona as an attempt to test Raskolnikov's right to destroy, namely: the violence which threatens to erupt again at the expense of Luzhin; Raskolnikov's inflexible insistence on having his own way, manifested in his determination, of which his mother now speaks, to marry his landlady's crippled daughter (VI, 166; III, ii) and his demand that Dunya reject Luzhin (VI, 178; III, iii); and his own rejection of all authority, parental and divine, implied by his coolness towards and alienation from his mother and by spurning of prayer once he feels secure (VI, 147; II, vii). But most importantly, self-will finds expression in his attitude towards crime, which now seems only a further logical consequence of the thorough rejection of all those 'constraints', 'prejudices' and 'traditions' execrated by Pisarev.

V

As Dostoyevsky deepens the examination of the implications of current radical theory, so he broadens his consideration of crime, or more correctly, as the Russian word *prestupleniye* implies, of transgression. He now broaches important questions concerning the general rules by which the conduct of all individuals in a society is circumscribed, namely the laws. There thus begins in his work that profound debate on the nature and status of law which culminates in his last novel and crowning achievement, *The Brothers Karamazov*.

The word 'law', of course, may have not only a juridical sense of a 'body of enacted or customary rules recognized by a community as binding', but also, among many others, a moral sense of 'precepts' or 'binding injunctions' to be followed because they are dictated by conscience rather than by statute; and, thirdly, a scientific sense of 'correct statement of invariable sequence between specified conditions and specified phenomenon'.[43] The variety of meanings inherent in the English word 'law' is also available in its Russian equivalent *zakon*, although in Soviet lexicography the moral sense tends to be either blurred, merging with the morally neutral concept of a 'generally accepted rule',[44] or simply classified as obsolete.[45]

Numerous Western jurists have discussed the relationship of law in its juridical sense (which may be known as 'human', 'positive' or 'temporal' law) to law in some broader and more abstract sense. They have considered whether there exists a 'natural law', that is, a system of right or justice held to be common to all mankind',[46] and have asked themselves whether human law is an expression of such 'natural law'. Does human law then embody some principles of absolute, universal and permanent validity, can it be evaluated against certain immutable standards? Or does it merely reflect the values and needs of a particular society, and therefore have little or no relevance in other times and places?[47] (The debate is analogous to that on the question as to whether moral values are absolute or relative.) Now Dostoyevsky, as a Russian Orthodox writer passionately critical of most tendencies in Western thought, cannot be closely identified with any Western exponents or opponents of theories of natural law, but he is pre-occupied with the sort of questions to which Western jurists have addressed themselves, and on one level *Crime and Punishment* represents his first major attempt to deal with them.

Law in its juridical sense—and it is with the 'juridical question' that Raskolnikov's remarks to Porfiry in part III begin (VI, 200; III, v); indeed Raskolnikov has been a student of this law—has little status for Dostoyevsky's anti-hero in his murderous frame of mind. It is clear that the concept lacks absolute authority for him, since he treats it in the same relativistic fashion as crime in part I and again in part III. All the great 'lawgivers' to whom he refers—the Spartan Lycurgus, the Athenian Solon, Mohammed and Napoleon (remembered in Russia not only as an invader but also as the promulgator of a new legal code on which Speransky largely based the code he was preparing for Alexander I)[48]—were at the same time 'criminals' by virtue of the fact that they destroyed orders sanctified by their forebears. Conversely, just as an act which might normally be deemed a crime was " 'not a crime' " when seen from Raskolnikov's utilitarian point of view in part I, so the infringement of a law by a Lycurgus might with a similar change of perspective be seen as the establishment of a law. Lawbreakers or 'destroyers' might also be designated 'lawgivers' and 'institutors' *(ustanoviteli)* of mankind (VI, 199–200; III, v).

Historically speaking, the view that human law had some absolute validity, derived from the existence of an immutable moral law which it expressed, was weakened by the promotion of law in its third, scientific, sense. For thinkers like Comte, who accepted only those concepts which could be verified empirically, rejected as obsolete unproven hypotheses about the existence of God or the nature of man on which moral law rested. They were interested not so much in assumptions about how man ought to behave as in the description and classification of the ways in which he in fact did behave. Again Darwin, in demonstrating scientifically the adaptability of organisms in the struggle for survival, provided a biological precedent for thinkers who urged institutional and legal change in response to external pressures.[49] In this respect, therefore, he too helped to undermine the view that legal orders rest on some permanently valid principle.

The Russian radical thinkers of the 1860s, much influenced by Comte, Darwin and other Western writers who adopted a supposedly scientific approach to the problems that interested them, also treated as absolute and binding only the empirically verifiable scientific law and rejected any intuited natural *laws.* They insisted that a rational man could acknowledge only the empirical method of enquiry which proceeded along the lines of Comte's 'positive philosophy' and treated 'all phenomena as subject to immutable natural law'.[50] Such laws as had already been discovered in the natural sciences they propagated with enthusiasm and every effort was made to reveal equally immutable laws in disciplines such as the study of man's behaviour and even his aesthetic concepts, which had not previously been considered amenable to scientific treatment. Thus Chernyshevsky assured his readers that 'all the diversity' in human motivation and in human life in general sprang 'from one and the same nature in accordance with one and the same law' and set out to investigate the 'laws in accordance with which the heart and the will operate'.[51] Pisarev's thought is coloured by the same admiration of the natural sciences and the same faith in the universal applicability of the scientific method.

It is clear from the way in which Raskolnikov frequently expresses his thoughts in *Crime and Punishment* that he too, like many other members of his generation, is a devotee of the scientific method. Just as the student has done in part I, he presents in part III a mathematical equation, in which the discoveries of Kepler and Newton are weighed against the lives of 'one, ten, a hundred and so forth people who might prevent this discovery or might stand in the way as an obstacle' (VI, 199; III, v). He neatly divides humanity into 'two categories' and repeats the terms 'first category' and 'second category' and expresses quali- fications parenthetically as if in a mathematical formula.[52] And towards the end of his monologue he uses an image already pop- ular with Dostoyevsky to evoke the scientific approach (XIX, 131; V, 104; II, iv), alluding to the 'retort' in which the processes he has described are taking place. He also says now that there must exist some 'law of nature' which determines the 'order of ap- pearance of people, of all these categories and subdivisions'. He is convinced that an exact law governs the divisions of men into the categories he has postulated: 'there certainly is and must be a definite law'. Nor does the fact that such a law has not yet been discovered shake Raskolnikov's conviction that 'it exists and may subsequently become known' (VI, 202; III, v).

In appealing to scientific law Raskolnikov is in effect arguing not only that people who have a new word to say will inevitably break the established criminal law, but also that such people will inevitably appear. This scientific explanation of lawbreaking in turn diminishes the status of any moral law from which human law might have derived some authority. For the scientific inevi- tability of lawbreaking tends to reduce the culpability of the law- breakers. A moral choice is valuable if there is freedom to make it. But if actions, in Büchner's words, are in the final analysis 'dependent upon a fixed necessity' and if therefore 'in every in- dividual case free choice has only an extremely limited, if any, sphere of action', then criminals 'are rather deserving of pity than of disgust'.[53] And the smaller the degree of control a man has over his actions, the smaller becomes the burden of guilt he must bear for them. The legal implications of this argument were clear to the positivist criminologists of the second half of the nine- teenth century, who 'instead of assuming a moral stance that focussed on measuring the criminal's "guilt" and "responsibility", . . . attempted a morally neutral and social interpretation of crime and its treatment'.[54] If crime was the result of abnormalities in the human organism or of inherited or environmental factors outside the control of the criminal, punishment was an inappropriate response to it. Raskolnikov himself, in invoking scientific law to confirm his right to kill, is brushing aside moral law and thereby detracting from his guilt: he seems, as the horrified Razumikhin notices (VI, 202–3; III, v), to permit the shedding of blood in accordance with the dictates of one's conscience, and he does not expect the 'extraordinary' man to suffer if he kills; indeed the greater the calculable utility of his act, the less significant will be the burden of moral responsibility he will bear (VI, 200; III, v).

The ascendancy of a scientific law, then, allows certain people to break the moral law as well as human law with impunity. Thus as law in one of its senses is promoted, so the status of law in another of its senses is diminished. The 'men of the sixties', who had shown such industry in redefining concepts and values such as the 'beautiful' and the 'good', had also shifted the emphasis of the concept of law from the morally binding to the scientifically inevitable. Indeed, in so far as the 'extraordinary' men are granted free will, it had become morally binding, Dostoyevsky implies, for them to promote what was scientifically indisputable. For the establishment of scientific laws seems in part III of *Crime and Punishment* to have become the most pressing moral obligation. Kepler and Newton, to whom Raskolnikov refers in support of his thesis that 'extraordinary people' may 'step over' certain 'obstacles' (VI, 199; III, v), are unaggressive scientists whose association in Raskolnikov's mind with Napoleon seems at first sight strange. In fact they constitute classic examples of the discoverers of physical laws of motion of the sort admired for their apparent incontestability by the men of the sixties. (Thus in *What Is To Be Done?* Newton is extolled by Rakhmetov as the 'most brilliant and the most sane mind of all the minds known to us'.)[55] And to Raskolnikov the promotion of the discoveries of these scientists had evidently seemed so important that what might normally have been designated a 'crime' could have been in a sense quite legitimately committed in order to assist it. Raskolnikov seems to imply by his choice of examples, then, that the cause of the transgression of the law may be the need to establish a scientific law and even that such a transgression is obligatory. For although in one breath he denies that he insists, as he thinks Porfiry has insinuated, that 'extraordinary people inevitably must and always were bound to commit all sorts of excesses', he does in the next admit that a Newton, encountering obstacles to the dissemination of his discoveries, 'would have the right, and would even be obliged . . . ' to eliminate the individuals standing in his way (VI, 199; III, v).[56]

VI

It is a repeatedly asserted or implied belief of Dostoyevsky's in the early 1860s that his radical contemporaries were wrong to concede omnicompetence to law in its scientific sense. By devising and upholding such law they neither provided an entirely accurate description of man's nature and conduct nor did they lay down sound rules about how he ought to behave.

Just as the observation of a utilitarian ethic tended to reduce to impersonal mathematical terms problems of human conduct which were properly speaking unquantifiable, so the attempt to bring all man's characteristics and behaviour under the jurisdiction of scientific laws resulted in an oversimplification of a very complex reality. In attempting to embrace reality in its entirety in some logically incontestable schema, the radicals failed properly to take into account aspects of man's being other than his reason; for phenomena which were not rational, or the existence of which could not be empirically demonstrated, did not seem to lend themselves to precise analysis. The exponents of the supposedly scientific doctrines, Dostoyevsky wrote in his notebook, were 'theoreticians' who wished to 'clip' man, to shear off him those parts of his being which did not accord with the soothing theories they had devised in the isolation of their studies or which might serve to obstruct the development of the utopias they envisaged.[57] There are references to such simplification in *Crime and Punishment* too: Razumikhin, for example, accuses the socialists of failing to take human nature into account when designing their phalansteries. 'All the mysteries of life' they try to accommodate 'on two printer's sheets' (VI, 197; III, v). In particular the radicals seemed to Dostoyevsky to ignore man's often irrational craving to assert his individuality, to preserve at least that illusion of free will so cherished by the Underground Man. They also failed to take into consideration conscience, the 'moral sense of right and wrong',[58] which might inhibit harsh treatment of one's fellows. Individual conscience, having no bearing on the general utility of an action, is not a faculty to which the student in part I of *Crime and Punishment* is prepared to devote serious attention (VI, 54; I, vi). And Raskolnikov, treating it more as an attribute of the oppressed mass than as an innate human characteristic, expects to remain free of the remorse it might arouse (VI, 203; III, v).

In opposition to the supposedly irrefutable scientific laws exalted by the radicals, Dostoyevsky puts forward certain laws of his own which seem to him more accurately to describe reality as he perceives it. There is a 'law of truth and human nature', he writes in his letter to Katkov, which leads the criminal voluntarily to accept 'torments'.[59] The suffering required by the criminal and described by Porfiry as a 'great thing' (VI, 352; VI, ii) contrasts with the pleasure which utilitarianism postulates as the only end of man's existence. It is a law of nature for Porfiry, moreover, that a criminal like Raskolnikov, pursued by psychological methods, and left at large in the uncertainty dreaded by the rationalist, will eventually trap himself (VI, 262; IV, v). And 'facts'—the investigator's equivalent of scientific data, which it is not really proper for him to question (VI, 346; VI, ii)—Porfiry treats with scepticism, for they may lead him into error no less than the 'abstract arguments of reason' which have so beguiled Raskolnikov (VI, 263; IV, v).

Not only does Dostoyevsky suggest the existence of psychological laws at variance with those accepted by the radicals (whose approach to psychology, as Dostoyevsky perceives it, is reflected in *Crime and Punishment* in the statements of Zosimov on the subject (e.g. VI, 159; III, i)). More importantly Dostoyevsky also reinstates the moral law which scientific law tended to ignore or to suppress. The moral law emanated not from the reason—only a 'twentieth part' of the Underground Man's capacity for living (V, 115; II, v)—but from the spiritual side of man's nature which, Chernyshevsky had categorically stated, did not exist.[60] In opposition to Chernyshevsky's supposedly scientific law, which asserted that egoism was the basic impulse of all human actions,[61] Dostoyevsky's moral law postulated in man a need for 'sacrifice', the submission of one's ego to others in selfless love.[62] It is clearly this law which Dostoyevsky believes will prevail in the final stage of human development, designated 'Christianity' and envisaged by him in plans for an article drafted shortly before he embarked on the writing of *Crime and Punishment*. The Christian phase would supplant and stand in opposition to a phase designated 'civilization', characterized by the extreme development of the individual consciousness and crowned by the advent of socialism.[63] And it is Christ's commandment 'Thou shalt love thy neighbour as thyself', observed in *Crime and Punishment* by Sonya, which ultimately prohibits acts based on the supposedly scientific precept approved by Luzhin, 'Love, above all, thyself alone' (VI, 116; II, v).

For Dostoyevsky the moral law, not any scientific law, is sovereign: there is 'one law—the moral law', he wrote in a rough draft of one of the scenes of the novel.[64] Beside this law human law pales into insignificance. Thus Porfiry, although he is the chief agent of the human law in *Crime and Punishment*, is manifestly 'less concerned with apprehending Raskolnikov as a criminal', as Richard Peace has aptly put it, 'than with saving him as a human being'.[65] In any case the '[juridical] punishment for a crime', Dostoyevsky wrote in his letter to Katkov, 'frightens a criminal much less than they [the lawgivers] think, in part because *he himself morally requires it*'.[66] But the unimportance of the human law beside the moral law does not entitle one to break it. For whereas the promotion of supposedly scientific laws tended to weaken existing legal codes by making crime a relative concept, the reinstatement of moral law strengthened them by making acts such as killing absolutely wrong. Raskolnikov therefore does not have the right to disregard human law on the grounds that its authority is threatened by inevitable political, social or intellectual change; on the contrary, he is bound to obey it because it expresses a higher Christian principle.

VII

The points I have made stand in need of three qualifications. Firstly, Dostoyevsky was not a single-minded publicist, like Chernyshevsky, but first and foremost an artist committed to faithful and full representation of reality as he perceived it; he did not therefore give definitive answers to the questions he posed. Secondly, some of the views implicit in *Crime and Punishment* were not fully developed by Dostoyevsky for more than another decade, until he presented that profound debate which takes place in *The Brothers Karamazov* on the relationship between the 'laws of Christ' and the laws of the state and on the need to punish the criminal by cutting off not a limb but a soul (XIV, especially 55–63; I, v). And thirdly, to read the novel primarily as a contribution to the intellectual life of the period is to illuminate it only partially and to leave out of consideration its artistic riches and other qualities.

Nevertheless it is true to say that Dostoyevsky, unlike Turgenev, did have passionate convictions which find expression in his novels. Moreover, Dostoyevsky's objections to the new radical *Weltanschauung* had on the whole become clear by the time he came to write *Crime and Punishment* in 1865. Most importantly, it was probably mainly out of a desire to state or at least to clarify these objections that Dostoyevsky now raised numerous important questions. Is man's behaviour determined by circumstances outside his control? Is he bound, if placed in certain conditions, to commit crime? Should criminals be considered blameless for their actions? Is it unjust that criminals should suffer punishment? Is the individual unimportant by comparison with the larger group to which he belongs? Do affirmative answers to these questions help to promote crime by destroying in the individual a sense of responsibility for his actions and love and respect for his fellows? And it is in no small measure from Dostoyevsky's examination of these questions—to which radical contemporaries seemed to give such crude and dogmatic answers—that *Crime and Punishment* derives its lasting and universal significance.

Notes

1. Dostoyevsky's reactions in the early 1860s to some of the views of the radicals are described in my article 'Dostoyevsky and Chernyshevsky', *Slavonic and East European Review,* 57 (1979), 509–30.

2. N. G. Chernyshevsky, 'Antropologicheskiy printsip v filosofii', in his *Polnoye sobraniye sochineniy* (Moscow, 1939–50), vol.7, p. 240.

3. See *PSS* VI, e.g. pp. 16 (Lewes), 197 (reference to phalanstery of French utopian socialists), 280 (Fourier and Darwin), 283 (Dobrolyubov).

4. The relationship of *Crime and Punishment* to current polemics in Russia has not been very fully examined except by Joseph Frank, 'The world of Raskolnikov', *Encounter,* 26 (June 1966), 30–35. See also Richard Peace, *Dostoyevsky: An Examination of the Major Novels* (Cambridge, 1971), pp. 19ff.

5. E.g. the nos. for October 1864, February 1865, March, May and November 1864.

6. See Dostoyevsky's *Zapisnyye knizhki,* published in *Literaturnoye nasledstvo,* 83 (1971), 219.

7. See Katharine Strelsky, 'Lacenaire and Raskolnikov', *Times Literary Supplement,* 8 January 1971, 47. The transcript of the trial and Dostoyevsky's preface to it were published in *Vremya,* February 1861.

8. N. G. Chernyshevsky, *Chto delat'?,* in his *Polnoye sobraniye sochineniy,* vol. 11, p. 175.

9. Robert Owen, *A New View of Society* (Harmondsworth, 1970), pp. 99, 104, 106, 125. Owen's italics.

10. L. Büchner, *Force and Matter* (London, 1864), p. 246.

11. Chernyshevsky, 'Antropologicheskiy printsip', p. 266.

12. N. A. Dobrolyubov, 'Tyomnoye tsarstvo', in his *Sobraniye sochineniy v devyati tomakh* (Moscow/Leningrad, 1961–64), vol. 5, p. 47.

13. See F.M. Dostoyevsky, *The Notebooks for 'Crime and Punishment',* ed. and trans. Edward Wasiolek (Chicago/London), 1967, p. 96 (*PSS,* VII, 71).

14. Rakhmetov comes to the fore in ch. 3, sections xxix and xxx of Chernyshevsky's novel; see esp. *Chto delat'?,* p. 207.

15. D. I. Pisarev maintained this point of view even in his review of *Crime and Punishment.* The cause of Raskolnikov's crime, he wrote, lay 'not

in his brain but in his pocket'. See Pisarev's article 'Bor'ba za zhizn'', in his *Sochineniya* (4 vols., Moscow, 1955–56), vol. 4, p. 324.

16. In particular see the discussion of *Crime and Punishment* in the light of classical utilitarian thought by A. D. Nuttall, *Crime and Punishment: Murder as Philosophic Experiment* (Edinburgh, 1978), esp. ch. 3.

17. The letter is reprinted in Dostoyevsky, *Pis'ma,* ed. A. S. Dolinin (Moscow/Leningrad, 1928–59), vol. 1, pp. 417–21.

18. Chernyshevsky, 'Antropologicheskiy printsip', p. 286.

19. 'Arithmetic' and 'mathematics' are mentioned even more frequently, in connection with utilitarian morality, in Dostoyevsky, *Notebooks* (e.g. pp. 48, 53, 58, 65, 67, 69, 70) than in the finished novel.

20. Chernyshevsky, 'Antropologicheskiy printsip', p. 254.

21. N. N. Strakhov's comment, cited in the notes to *Crime and Punishment* in Dostoyevsky's *Sobraniye sochineniy* (Moscow, 1956–68), vol. 5, p. 590. Dostoyevsky himself talks in similar terms in his letter to Katkov (Dostoyevsky, *Pis'ma,* vol. 1, p. 418).

22. A lengthy examination of this polemic is contained in B. P. Koz'min's article, " 'Raskol v nigilistakh' ", reprinted in his collected works under the title *Iz istorii revolyutsionnoy mysli v Rossii* (Moscow, 1961), pp. 20–67. See also Frank, 'World of Raskolnikov'. On the book by Napoleon, see the notes in Dostoyevsky, *Sobraniye sochineniy,* vol. 5, pp. 582–83, and Peace, *Dostoyevsky,* p. 24.

23. 'Gospodin Shchedrin, ili raskol v nigilistakh', *Epokha,* May 1865.

24. E.g. the nos. for March 1864, pp. 339–43, and October 1864, pp. 1–9.

25. Peace, *Dostoyevsky,* p. 29.

26. Pisarev, 'Myslyashchiy proletariat', *Sochineniya,* vol. 4, pp. 7–49.

27. N. G. Chernyshevsky, *Esteticheskiye otnosheniya iskusstva k deystvitel'nosti,* in his *Polnoye sobraniye sochineniy,* vol. 2, pp. 5–92.

28. Pisarev, 'Razrusheniye estetiki', *Sochineniya,* vol. 3, pp. 418–35.

29. Pisarev, 'Skholastika XIX veka', *Sochineniya,* vol. 1. p. 103.

30. Ibid., pp. 120, 122.

31. Dostoyevsky, *Zapisnyye knizhki,* p. 151. See also p. 167n.

32. Pisarev, 'Realisty', *Sochineniya,* vol. 3, pp. 7–138.

33. I. S. Turgenev, *Ottsy i deti,* in his *Polnoye sobraniye sochineniy i pisem* (28 vols., Moscow/Leningrad, 1960–68), vol. 8, p. 243.

34. Pisarev, 'Bazarov', *Sochineniya,* vol. 2, p. 11.

35. Ibid., pp. 9ff.

36. T. G. Masaryk, *The Spirit of Russia* (London, 1919), vol. 2, p. 105.

37. It is perhaps significant that Dostoyevsky was one of the very few

people whom Turgenev considered to have really understood *Ottsy deti* (see Turgenev, *Pis'ma*, vol. 4, pp. 358–59, in *Polnoye sobraniye sochineniy*).

38. Pisarev, 'Bazarov', *Sochineniya*, vol. 2, pp. 15, 20–21.

39. Chernyshevsky, *Chto delat'?*, e.g., p. 227.

40. Bazarov in ch. 21 tells Arkady: 'iz menya lopukh rasti budet'. Arkady's surname, of course, is Kirsanov.

41. Chernyshevsky, *Chto delat'?*, p. 195. The expression 'people of the future' also became commonplace; it appears in the title of an article, 'Lyudi budushchego i geroi meshchanstva', published in 1868, by P. N. Tkachev, a revolutionary disciple of Pisarev, who had at one time contributed to Dostoyevsky's journal, *Time*. In this article Tkachev argues that the end (the happiness of mankind in socialist society) justifies means which may involve the transgression of commonly accepted morality. See his *Izbrannyye sochineniya na sotsial'no-politicheskiye temy* (Moscow, 1932–36), vol. 1, pp. 173–233).

42. Dostoyevsky, *Notebooks*, p. 188 (*PSS*, VI, 155).

43. The meanings cited are given in the *Oxford English Dictionary*, 5th ed. (Oxford, 1974).

44. S.I. Ozhegov, *Slovar' russkogo yazyka*, 8th ed. (Moscow, 1970).

45. *Slovar' sovremennogo russkogo literaturnogo yazyka* (17 vols., Moscow Leningrad, 1950–65), vol. 4.

46. See the entry on 'natural law' in *Encyclopaedia Britannica*, 15th ed., *Macropaedia*, vol. 12, p. 863.

47. Ibid., pp. 863–65; see also the entry on 'Western philosophy of law' (Ibid., *Macropaedia*, vol. 10, pp. 716–19).

48. See Marc Raeff, *Michael Speransky: Statesman of Imperial Russia* (The Hague, 1957), pp. 68–69.

49. *Encyclopaedia Britannica, Macropaedia*, vol. 10, p. 717.

50. Auguste Comte, *Cours de philosophie positive*, in his *Oeuvres* (Paris, 1968–71), vol. 1, pp. 11–12. Comte's italics.

51. Chernyshevsky, 'Antropologicheskiy printsip', pp. 283, 292; see also his *Esteticheskiye otnosheniya*, p. 6.

52. Compare the similarly mathematical syntax of D-503, when he is confident that all phenomena are comprehensible and explicable, in the early stages of Zamyatin's novel *My*.

53. Büchner, *Force and Matter*, pp. 240, 246.

54. See the entry on 'criminology' in *Encyclopaedia Britannica, Macropaedia*, vol. 5, p. 283.

55. Chernyshevsky, *Chto delat'?*, p. 197.

56. The pause indicated by the dots after the word 'obliged' in Raskolnikov's monologue seems to emphasize that he himself is aware that he is no longer talking about the possibility of transgressing but about the necessity or inevitability of doing so.

57. E.g. Dostoyevsky, *Zapisnyye knizhki,* p. 154. See also section III of my article 'Dostoyevsky and Chernyshevsky', *Slavonic and East European Review,* LVII, 4, 1979, pp. 309–30.

58. *Oxford English Dictionary,* 5th ed.

59. Dostoyevsky, *Pis'ma,* vol. 1, p. 419.

60. Chernyshevsky, 'Antropologicheskiy printsip', p. 240.

61. Ibid., p. 282.

62. Dostoyevsky, *Zapisnyye knizhki,* p. 175.

63. Ibid., pp. 246–48.

64. Dostoyevsky, *Notebooks,* p. 58 (*PSS,* VI, 142).

65. Peace, *Dostoyevsky,* p. 44.

66. Dostoyevsky, *Pis'ma,* vol. 1, p. 419. Square brackets enclose words written above the line in Dostoyevsky's manuscript.

"The Other World" in
Crime and Punishment

V. E. VETLOVSKAYA

✦ ✦ ✦

HAVING COMMITTED THE CRIME and killed the old money-lender, Raskolnikov, as we know, not only killed her, but himself. Talking to Sonya, the hero himself stresses this last circumstance, giving it prominence: "Did I murder the old woman? I killed myself, not that old creature! There and then I did for myself at one blow, for ever! . . . But it was the devil who killed the old hag, not I . . ." [402].[1] Sonya reacts to Raskolnikov's admission in the same sense:

> Suddenly, as if she had been stabbed, she started, cried out, and flung herself, without knowing why, on her knees in front of him.
> "What have you done, what have you done to yourself?" she said despairingly, and, starting up, threw herself on his neck. . . . [394]

But, of course, suicide and murder are here one and the same "deed"; and if the devil at the hands of Raskolnikov dealt with the old woman, then it was also he who helped the hero "do

149

for" himself along with her. Characteristic motifs accompanying the crime from the very beginning depict the hero, having committed himself to the evil "deed", both as an executioner and as victim. Thus, when he has heard by chance that Lizaveta would not be home and the old woman *"would be at home alone"* [59], Raskolnikov returns to his room "like a man condemned to death" [59]:

> His reactions during this last day, which had come upon him so unexpectedly and settled everything at one stroke, were almost completely mechanical, as though someone had taken his hand and pulled him along irresistibly, blindly, with supernatural strength and without objection. It was as if a part of his clothing had been caught in the wheel of a machine and he was being dragged into it. [67–8]

"So it is true"—Raskolnikov thinks, as he goes along with the axe obligingly put in his way by the "devil" [69], and submitting himself in effect to his unnatural power—"that men going to execution are passionately interested in any object they chance to see on the way" [70]. In the scene where he waits by the locked door the criminal in no way differs from his victim: "Someone was standing silently just inside the door and listening, just as he was doing outside holding her breath and probably also with her ear to the door" [71]. The fear which, one would think, only the victim would experience seizes the murderer too:

> The old woman threw a glance at it [the pledge], but then immediately fixed her eyes on those of her uninvited guest. She looked at him attentively, ill-naturedly, and mistrustfully. A minute or so went by; he even thought he could see a glint of derision in her eyes, as if she had guessed everything. He felt that he was losing his nerve and was frightened, so frightened that he thought if she went on looking at him like that, without a word, for even half a minute longer, he would turn tail and run away. [72]

A little later, and stained with the blood he has spilt, Raskolnikov listens in terror to the footsteps of a person coming up to his apartment. The murderer is in the position of the victim, for whom, in contrast to himself, it seems danger no longer holds any terror:

> They were coming here! Suddenly he felt as if he had turned to stone, like a sleeper who dreams that he is being hotly pursued and threatened with death, and finds himself rooted to the spot, unable to stir a finger.
>
> At length, when the footsteps had begun the last flight, he started to life, and just managed to slip swiftly and dexterously back from the landing into the flat and close the door behind him. Then he grasped the bolt and slid it gently, without a sound, into its socket. Instinct had come to his aid. When he had done, he stayed quiet, holding his breath, close to the door. The unknown visitor was also at the door. They were standing now, opposite one another, as he and the old woman had stood with the door dividing them, when he had listened there a short time ago. [78–79]

But now nothing separates the criminal and the victim: they are locked in by the same bolt and are on the same side of the door, whatever the door may be that this bolt locks—whether it be the old woman's apartment which Raskolnikov from now on (after what, in the words of Svidrigaylov, he "had been up to there" [*nakurolesil*] [465]) he has grounds to consider his own (and therefore later attempts to "rent" it [165–168]) or his own pitiful closet, in which, however small it may be, the old woman also has good grounds to take up residence:

> "Who's fastened the door then? See, he's taken to locking his door now! Does he think someone's going to run off with him? Open the door, my lad; wake up!"
> "What do they want? Why is the porter here? They must have found out. Shall I resist, or shall I open the door? Better open it! Damnation! . . ."
> He half rose, stretched forward, and undid the hook. The room was so small that it was possible to do this without leaving his bed. [87]

Apropos the bolt; apparently, for Porfiry, the unlocked door during the crime was also a "trait", which, given the totality of circumstantial indications, suggested a real piece of evidence:

> "No, Rodion Romanovich, I am not mistaken. I have my scrap of proof. I had found it even then; God sent it to me!"
> "What proof?"
> "I shall not tell you, Rodion Romanovich." [439]

Compare the words he uttered shortly before: " 'There is resolution evident here, for the first step, [...] a resolve like that of a man falling from a precipice or flinging himself off a tower; this is the work of a man carried along into crime, as it were, by some outside force. He forgot to shut the door behind him' " [437]. And earlier: " 'I have been here before, the day before yesterday, in the evening; did you know? [...] I came up and found the room open; I looked round—I waited a while. I went away without even telling the servant I had called. Don't you lock your door?' " [429–430].

And again:

> They all went out together.
> "Aren't you going to fasten the door?" asked Razumikhin, descending the steps behind them.
> "I never do ... Though I've been meaning to buy a lock for two years," he added carelessly. "They are fortunate people who have nothing to lock up, aren't they?" he said to Sonya, laughing. [232–233]

But Raskolnikov himself no longer belongs to the "fortunate people": after the crime he has committed he has something to shut up and shut up about—in contrast to Mikolka, who, as Porfiry is convinced, will still "open up"[2]—take back his statements and recant the guilt of another which he has taken on [436]. In a certain sense the hero is now more or less always on the hook and behind the bolt, whether he closes the door or leaves it ajar. Cf.:

He leaned as near as possible to Zametov and began moving his lips, but no sound came from them; they remained like this for half a minute. He knew what he was doing, but he could not restrain himself. A terrible word trembled on his lips, as the bolt had trembled *then* on the door: now, now, the bolt will give way; now, now, the word will slip out; oh, only to say it!

"And what if it was I who killed the old woman and Lizaveta?" he said suddenly, and—came to his senses. [159] (cf. [154–155])

But, following his former custom, the hero, too, (and at the most critical moment), did not lock up, not that he couldn't, but he actually forgot, just as he forgot about his hat which was "ridiculous" and "too noticeable" [3, 69]. The devil who controlled Raskolnikov's judgement and will [59], in leading him to the "execution", forced him, with a certain malicious mockery, to overlook these trifles, and he twice "blundered".[3] "The devil is in the detail",[4] we may say, suggesting the insidious nature of this forgetfulness. For, if the first slip, for all its obvious ability to attract attention, remained unobserved by anybody, then the second slip had fatal consequences: it pushed the hero into yet another murder, completely unnecessary in his calculations: had the door been locked, Lizaveta would not have entered without a sound.

But let us return to the scene of the crime, where Raskolnikov, having performed the role of executioner, in a more or less considered fashion, suddenly and unexpectedly, finds himself behind a locked door in the guise of victim: " 'Are they fast asleep in there, or dead, or what, confound them?' the visitor [Koch] boomed in a resounding voice.[. . .] 'Oh, confound it all, they must be asleep or something!' " [79]. Koch's "they" includes all those on the other side of the door from him—the old woman, Lizaveta and Raskolnikov himself, deprived of breath by the same noose of the axe and then that of the bolt (Remember: "He stayed quiet, holding his breath" [78]) and plunged into a terrible dream ("like a sleeper who dreams that he is being hotly pursued and threatened with death") and later, "Everything seemed to be happening in a dream" [79]. But here, apart from the old woman, Lizaveta and Raskolnikov, there is yet another figure, who, in contrast to them not only does not sleep, but, as is well known, does not even nod—that is the devil.

He has been with Raskolnikov all the time. He knows everyone and everything. Cf. " 'Isn't anybody in?' cried the new arrival in loud and cheerful tones [. . .] 'The devil only knows . . . ' (ibid.). And later: 'The old witch fixed a time with me herself [. . .] And where the devil she can have got I don't know' " [80]. But, in fact, this is understandable, because where would a witch loaf off to, if not to the devil—to him alone. But there is no need for her to go far, she has no need at all to stir, for the devil is close by. It is not by chance that every now and again he is mentioned in this scene:

"What the devil? . . . "
The time was passing [. . .]
"Oh, the devil! . . . " he [Koch—V.V.] exclaimed impatiently, abandoning his watch and starting to hurry downstairs[. . .]
"Oh, God, what am I to do?"
Raskolnikov took off the bolt [. . .] and went downstairs. He had gone down three flights when a great commotion broke out below him. Where could be go? There was no-where to hide. He was on the point of running back to the flat.
"Hi, stop! You devil! Just wait!" [81]

It is clear from this sequence of motifs, that the devil has direct relevance for Raskolnikov. However, what follows introduces a degree of correction and more precision: "Down below someone tore out of a flat shouting and did not so much run as tumble down the stairs, yelling at the top of his voice:

"Mitka! Mitka! Mitka! Mitka! Devil take you !"[5] [ibid.]

It turns out that the devil *has been called Mitka*; in other words [according to a Russian idiom—ED.][6] at the most anxious and painful moment for the hero he has disappeared.[7] "Serving" Ras-

kolnikov in their "joint deed" [61] the devil has left the hero to
pay for this "deed" alone, and pay the full price; for in pledging
the little board and its iron plate with the witch, at the same
time the hero was pledging his soul to the devil. From this comes
the belated fear of Raskolnikov for signing receipts even for lawful
money. For all these "receipts" are finally entered into one and
the same "book"—the book of his own life and fate. Cf.:

> "He'll manage to scribble it somehow. What's that you've
> got, a receipt-book?"
> "Yes, sir, here it is, sir."
> "Give it here [...]"
> "I don't want it," said Raskolnikov, pushing away the pen.
> "You don't want what?"
> "I am not going to sign."
> "What the devil?—A receipt is absolutely necessary."
> "I don't want ... the money ..."
> "Oh, it's the money you don't want, is it? Now there dear
> fellow, you lie, as I can bear witness!" [114]

In fact, Razumikhin can confirm that Raskolnikov was very
much in need of money, and although "after *that*" [105–107] Raskolnikov went to Razumikhin for money, he had gone to see
him with the same aim before *that*: " 'Hm ... [...] I will go to
see Razumikhin, of course ... but—not now. I will go to him
the day after, when *that* is over and done with and everything is
different' " [50]. Without knowing it, the money and the objects
which Raskolnikov took—not from Razumikhin, but from the
witch—he had already signed for with the devil—with his own
and others' sweat, with his own and others' blood. Cf.: " 'But
what makes you so pale? And your hands are trembling. Are you
ill[8] or something?' " [73], and later: "But his racking anxieties had
taken so much out of him that he could hardly move. Sweat
poured out of him; his neck was quite wet. 'You've had a drop
too much!' someone called after him as he came out on the
canal" [82–83]. As to the pact with the devil confirmed by this
receipt, it was drawn up earlier—during the hero's day-dreaming

and delirium in a corner, during those mathematical computations and calculations of his, justifying limitless presumptions to greatness, and along with them—sin and crime. To Raskolnikov these computations and calculations seemed beyond reproach: ". . . his analysis, in the sense of a moral solution of the question, was concluded; his casuistry had the cutting edge of a razor, and he could no longer find any conscious objections in his own mind" [67], whereas "all the analysis" was undertaken with a clouded mind, and deluded by the devil. Cf. earlier: " 'Lord!' he prayed, 'show me the way, that I may renounce this accursed fantasy of mine!' [. . .] It was as though the sore that had festered in his heart for a month had burst at last. Freedom! He was free now from the evil spells, from the sorcery and fascination, from the temptation" [57]. And later: " 'By the way, Sonya, when I used to lie there in the dark thinking of all this, was that the devil confounding me, eh?' " [401]. Cf. "All devils attempt at first to cloud our mind, and then suggest what they want: for if the mind does not close its eyes, then our treasure will not be stolen."[9] Cf. also: "Heed not the crafty serpent, which plays a variety of tricks upon us with the help of our passions, transforming itself into the Angel of light, and transforming things into what they are not, showing darkness as light, bitterness as sweetness." And further:

> . . . Look [. . .] what care and zeal the devil shows; as he 'as a roaring lion walketh about, seeking whom he may devour' [Peter, I, 5, 8], whom to seize as a prize, either in part or in whole. For when he seizes someone in part, he is not content with this, but all the time reaches out for something worse, until he has caused a sinful death—namely: at first he attempts to make us accept temptation, and then, that we conceive something bad in our hearts. Thus defiling and contaminating our soul, he tempts it to exceed the bounds of nature, and makes it full of folly [. . .] and blind, striving towards that, towards which it should not strive: to darkness instead of light; to bitterness instead of sweetness; to death instead of life.[10]

There are four levels of sin which constantly try to possess the heart and thought of man: "to think of sin, to agree with such thought, to express sinful thought in words; and the fourth—to carry out such thought in deed. In the latter case, the wrath of God cannot be averted."[11]

It is precisely because the devil already possessed a sufficiently reliable receipt and the pledge that he could allow himself to be absent—partly through volition, partly through compulsion (in as much as it was not he that Raskolnikov called on in a time of crisis (cf.: "O Lord, what shall I do!"))—to be absent, in order that immediately after this momentary absence he could immediately launch into a "new life" with his hero. Cf.: " 'What if it is beginning already? Can this be the beginning of my punishment? Look, over there!—I thought so!' Indeed, the frayed scraps of fringe he had cut off his trousers lay scattered on the floor in the middle of the room for everyone to see. 'But what can be the matter with me?' he wailed again like a lost soul" [86]. And then, when Raskolnikov has already "covered his tracks" and carefully destroyed all "evidence": " 'Oh, the devil take it all!' he thought in a sudden access of ungovernable irritation. 'If it's begun, it's begun, and to the devil with her, and with the new life!' " [104], and, of course, he is with it, with this "new life", because it was for its sake that the devil was so "obliging" to the hero [61].

Later Raskolnikov tells Sonya: " 'Sonya! I wanted to prove only one thing to you, that the devil was pulling me along then, [to the crime, to the "common deed"—V.V.] and that he made it clear to me after that, that I had not the right to travel by that road, because I am just as much a louse as everybody else! He had a good laugh at me, and now I have come to you! Take me in! If I were not a louse, would I have come to you?' " [402]. The question why he came to Sonya is not as simple as the hero thinks. But the fact that the devil has laughed at him is quite right.

Tempting him with the dream of quick and easy gain, the devil has turned that "capital" which Raskolnikov attempted to acquire with such pain into nothing, into absolute rubbish.[12] Cf.:

"I suppose you want all the capital straight off?"
He looked at her [Nastasya—V.V.] strangely and paused for
a moment.
"Yes, I do," he answered firmly.
"Well, you'd better go slow, or you'll frighten me; in fact
I'm frightened already." [27]

And later:

"What's that in your hand?"
He looked down; in his right hand he was still holding the
fringe he had cut off; the sock, and the torn pieces of his
pocket. He had slept with them like that. Afterwards, thinking about it, he remembered that when he half woke in his
fevered state, he had clutched them tightly in his fingers
and so fallen asleep again.
"Look, he's collected a handful of rags and taken them to
bed with him as if they were something precious . . ." And
Nastasya broke into one of her painfully violent fits of
laughter He whisked everything under the greatcoat and
stared fixedly at her. [87–88]

And again:

"Did I say anything when I was delirious?"
"Of course you did. You were out of your mind."
"What did I say?" [. . .]
"You're repeating yourself, you know. Are you worrying
about some secret or other? Don't be afraid; the Countess
was never mentioned. But you talked about some bulldog,
about ear-rings, and a chain, and Krestovsky Island [. . .].
Besides that, you were very interested in your own sock,
very. You were whining: 'Give it me, that's all I want.'
Zametov himself looked for your socks everywhere, and
handed you that rubbish with his own fair hands, washed
in scent and covered with rings. Only then did you calm
down, and you held the rubbish in your hand for days
together; we couldn't get it away from you.[. . .] And then
again you asked for the fringe from your trousers, and so

tearfully! We questioned you about it: what sort of fringe did you mean? But we couldn't make anything out...." [119–120]

The devil did not just rob the hero down to the last fringe and thread, he plundered him in a more capital way, taking away a life, which, up to a certain point, in the eyes of Raskolnikov had no particular value, but later turned out to be of enormous wealth even on a "small scale in space",[13] and making an attempt on his soul.

> Such is the guile of the devil. Those who trust in him he leads beyond the boundaries laid down for us by God, as though we could have much more [...] and seducing us with such hopes and depriving us of God's grace, he not only does not tell us anything further [...] but does not allow us to return to the former boundaries, within which we were safe, but he forces us to wander everywhere and nowhere lets us stop. It was this that led the first created man to his expulsion from paradise. Giving him hope of greater knowledge and respect, the devil deprived him even of that, which he had previously enjoyed in peace. Man not only did not become the equal of God, as the devil promised him, but fell under the yoke of death ... [14]

Raskolnikov found himself in a similar position when he did the "deed" which was his, and not his, and killed both others and himself.

In accordance with the logic of this situation the hero cannot in any way remain fully alive. After the first murder he "went dead" (although he was not very well from the very beginning, i.e. before the crime, though, of course, there was a connection[15]): "A footstep sounded in the room where the old woman lay. He stopped and remained motionless as the dead ..." [76]. And the second murder, it goes without saying, cannot bring him to life:

> "Hadn't I better slip into some gateway and wait on a staircase? No, that would be disastrous! Oughtn't I to get rid of the axe? What about taking a cab? ... A fatal blunder!"

At last he reached a side-street and, half dead, turned into it. [82]

After several hours spent in delirium, in feverish (and not just feverish) heat and cold [84, 87] Raskolnikov decides: "to go out somewhere and [. . .] this minute without a moment's delay" throw away all the rags splashed with blood, but:

> Once more a sudden chill congealed his blood [. . .] Several times he tried to tear himself from his couch and get up, but he could not do it. Finally he was awakened by a loud knocking on his door.
> "Open the door! You're not dead, are you? He's always fast asleep!" cried Nastasya, beating on the door with her fist.
> "Lying there fast asleep all day like a dog!" [. . .]
> "Perhaps he's not at home," said a man's voice.
> "Ah! That's the porter . . . What does he want?" [86–87]

The scene clearly has much in common with the one that took place at the old woman's door; it is as though the porter, whom Pestryakov, and then Koch, had gone to fetch ("I'll tell you what; let's go to the porter and get him to rouse them." [80]) had finally appeared. And although, as a rule, Nastasya says that Raskolnikov generally sleeps for whole days, this time, for the first time locking himself into his closet on the hook, he sleeps in a different way—he sleeps like a dead man. Therefore, in reply to Nastasya's question he might not be able to say either yes or no, just as he might not with full confidence reject the porter's supposition. The hero is alive and not alive. He is at home and not at home.

The motif *neither alive, nor dead*, or more accurately *still alive* and *already dead* marks the border where Raskolnikov's "new life" begins. It finds its expression in that the hero is now at one and the same time in this world and in the next. Having allowed himself to step over a certain line, Raskolnikov, against his own expectations, has stepped far further than he might have wished, and has stepped beyond the bounds of the living world.[16] This is the chief consequence of his "deed", unforeseen in any calculation. But there is nothing amazing here: if the beginning of our actions, and the actions themselves, lie within our will (thus Raskolnikov could agree or not agree with a sinful thought, act in accordance with it, or not act), then what results does not depend on us. Cf. the saying of the Venerable Maxim the Confessor: "All our good and bad deeds depend on our arbitrary will. What is not in our power are punishments and misfortunes; equally, too, their opposites."[17]

Belonging to another world sharply marks out the hero from the milieu of living people. Hence the freezing, otherworldly coldness which seizes hold of Raskolnikov immediately after the murder, and which later lays siege to him again and again. Hence his indifference, his emptiness:

> If he had heard himself condemned to be burnt at this moment he would hardly have stirred.[. . .] Something new and unexpected, something hitherto unknown and undreamt of, had taken place in him. He did not so much understand with his mind as feel instinctively with the full force of his emotions that he could never again communicate with these people in a great gush of feeling, as he had just now, or in any way whatever. Even if they had been his own brothers and sisters, instead of police officers, it would still have been impossible for him to turn to them [. . .]. He had never in his life before experienced so strange and desolating a feeling. [98]

Of course Raskolnikov was a lonely figure even earlier: "He had resolutely withdrawn from all human contacts, like a tortoise retreating into its shell, until the sight even of the face of the servant-girl who was supposed to look after him, and who looked in on him from time to time, made him shudder with revulsion" [25–26]. But his loneliness at that time was entirely voluntary; if he wanted to, Raskolnikov could come out of it without much effort [8]. However that "painful feeling" of profound alienation from each and everyone, which he felt in the police office [98], was no longer under his control. Even in the future it persecutes the hero. The very first attempt to turn to a good, intelligent and responsive human being, which for anyone else would present no difficulties, ends in failure for Raskolnikov: "When he came up to Razumikhin's room he had somehow not thought of how he would have to come face to face with him. Now it had taken him only a moment's trial to realize that he was less inclined than ever [and, it later becomes clear, not just on this occasion; cf. pp. 120–21, 123, 125, 146–47, 148 among others—V.V.] to enter into personal relations with anybody on the face of the earth" [105–106]. At the same time to see another's face is a consolation even in the torment of hell:

> As Father Makarii used to relate: "one day going through the desert, I found the skull of a dead man lying on the ground. When I struck the skull with a stave of palm, it said something to me. 'Who are you?' I asked. The skull replied 'I was the chief priest of idols and of the pagans who lived in this place, but you, Makarii, are a bearer of the spirit. When you take pity on those suffering in torment, and begin to pray for them, they feel some solace'. The elder asked 'What kind of solace, what torment?' and [the skull] says to him: 'By as much as the heavens are distant from the earth, by so much is there fire beneath us, and we stand amid fire from head to foot. It is impossible for any of us to see another face to face. The face of one is turned to the back of another. But when you pray for us, then each one, to some extent, sees the face of another. That is what our solace is.' "[18]

Such solace arises through kinship, through a sense of community uniting those languishing in the torment of hell. But, on the other hand, a certain sense of kinship and community undoubtedly unites living people too, and if Raskolnikov finds no solace in seeing another person, or persons, and is not inclined: "to come face to face with anybody at all in the world", it means that, in reality, he is too removed from this world and those in it. The hero scarcely senses them; even, perhaps, not at all; scarcely responds, or not at all, as though he had become deaf and dumb, as though his living, native language had suddenly become strange to him:

Without a word Raskolnikov picked up the sheets of German and the three roubles, and went out. Razumikhin looked after him in surprise. Raskolnikov [. . .] turned abruptly on his heel [. . .] laid the papers and the money on the table, still without a word, and was gone.

"You must be raving mad or something," roared Razumikhin, losing his temper at last [. . .] "What the devil did you come for, anyhow?"

"I don't want . . . translations . . ." muttered Raskolnikov, already half-way downstairs.

"Then what the deuce do you want?" cried Razumikhin from above. Raskolnikov went on down in silence.

"Hi, you! Where do you live?"

There was no answer. "Well then devil take you!"

He was on the Nikolaevsky Bridge before he came to himself again [. . .] The driver of a carriage laid his whip heavily across his back, because he had almost fallen under the horses' feet, in spite of the coachman's repeated cries. The blow so enraged him that, leaping for the parapet [. . .] he ground his teeth viciously with a clicking noise. [107–108]

It is precisely here on the bridge that he recalls his usual impression of the "superb panorama", which surrounds him. The "deaf and voiceless spirit" which this "splendid picture" always inspired in him was already with him and in him, wherever the hero might now live, or more accurately, wherever he might find himself.[19]

It appeared to him strange and marvellous that he should have stopped in that very same place as he used to do [. . .] In some gulf far below him, almost out of sight beneath his feet, lay all his past, all his old ideas, and problems, and thoughts, and sensations, and this great panorama and his own self, and everything, everything . . . He felt as if he had soared upwards and everything had vanished from his sight . . . He made an involuntary gesture with his hand, and became aware of the twenty-copeck piece squeezed in his fist [the very one he had just been given "in the name of

Christ"—V.V.]. He unclasped his hand and stared at the money, then flung it into the water [. . .] He felt that he had in that moment cut himself from everybody and everything, as if with a knife. [108–109]

The hero already consciously (but once again not without the aid of evil forces whose "every effort is to plunge you into despair as soon as you fall")[20] cuts the traces that link him with people and his former life, and along with a twenty-copeck piece buries them in the water. It does not mean, however, that in reality he succeeds in burying them.

In paradoxical fashion it turns out that the nearer the world of the dead is to the hero, the stranger and more dead the world of the living seems to him: "The crowd was dispersing, the police were still busy with the woman, someone shouted a reference to the police-station. . . . Raskolnikov had looked on with a strange feeling of indifference and detachment [. . .] His heart was empty and numb" [164]. And later: " 'Well, shall I go, I wonder, or not?' [to the police, in order to make a confession—V.V.] thought Raskolnikov, stopping in the middle of the road at a crossing and looking round as if he expected to hear the deciding word from somebody. But no response came from any quarter; everything was blank and dead, like the stones he trod on, dead for him, and for him alone . . ." [168].

"Dead" because he himself is dead, and from this later comes the motif of resurrection (see, for example, [300, 401] etc.). From this comes his forgetfulness and the obvious incongruity of his words and actions (a pervasive motif of his madness of his "confused mind") which people notice with an uncomfortable feeling, as soon as they come into contact with the hero, who has almost lost all connection with them:

"You still love her" [the landlady's daughter—V.V.], said Pulkheria Alexandrovna, moved.
"Her? Still? Oh, yes . . . you are talking of her! No. That might all belong to another world . . . and it is a long time ago. Yes, and everything round me seems as if it were hap-

pening somewhere else. [. . .] Even you . . . it is as if I were
looking at you from a thousand miles away. . . ." [221–222]

Just after this admission the hero's "closet" [*kamorka*] (it is also a
"cupboard" [*shkaf*], "coop" [*kletushka*], a "trunk" [*sunduk*], a "ship's
cabin" [*morskaia kaiuta*][21]) is called for the first time a "coffin":

> "What a dreadful room you have, Rodya, just like a coffin,"
> said Pulkheria Alexandrovna, breaking the oppressive silence
> [. . .]
> "Room?" said he absently. "Yes, the room made a big con-
> tribution . . . I've thought of that too . . . But if you knew
> what a strange idea you have just expressed, mama!" he
> added abruptly, with a mysterious smile. [222]

For the hero the comparison made by his mother has too direct
and bitter a meaning (cf. later [229]).

In this "coffin", in this "ship's cabin", Raskolnikov "voyages"
[*voiazhiruet*], both when he lies[22] there, and when he leaves it and
"gets up to something".[23] For even awake, he continues to sleep;
cf. the words of Razumikhin: " 'Don't worry, please, this is only
because he . . . is wandering again. He is quite capable of that even
when he is wide awake . . . ' " [114], and later the words of Svidrigaylov:

> "You are very transparent, Rodion Romanovich.[. . .] You
> come out of the house with your head held high. After
> twenty paces it is beginning to droop and your hands are
> folded behind your back. Your eyes are open, but obviously
> you see nothing of what is in front of you or all round. At
> last your lips begin to move and you talk to yourself, [. . .]
> and then finally you stand still for quite a time in the
> middle of the road. This is very bad. Perhaps somebody else
> notices you, besides me, and it won't do you any good".
> [448]

"No good", because Raskolnikov all too patently "betrays" himself
as being in a special category—the category of a man "not of this
world". Cf. Dunechka's impression later [467].

"Do you know that I am being followed?" asked Raskolni-
kov, looking searchingly at him.
"No, I don't know anything about it," [. . .]
"Well, let us leave me in peace," frowningly muttered Ras-
kolnikov.
"Very well, we will leave you in peace". [448]

Whether acting feverishly or in remaining in a death-like
peace,[24] Raskolnikov "voyages" [*voyazhiruet*] in the direction that
Svidrigaylov had moved before him, (cf. his "*voyazh*" to America)
in the direction of the other world and then disappearing in the
other world.[25] We must stress the motif of "America", so characteristic in this respect, which, before it resounds on the lips of
Svidrigaylov, first appears in the musings of Raskolnikov: " 'But
what is this? Am I still delirious, or is all this real? It seems real
enough . . . Ah, I remember: I must run away, run away at once;
I must, I absolutely must, fly. But . . . where? [. . .] I will take the
money and go away, and take other lodgings, where I shall not
be found . . . [. . .] They'll find me! [. . .]. It would be better to
run away altogether . . . a long way . . . to America' " [121].

Cf. later the advice of Svidrigaylov: " 'You'd better be off at once
to America somewhere. Run away young man! Perhaps there is
still time' " [466]. Up to the moment when Svidrigaylov suggests
that Raskolnikov should escape to America, the young man has
already had time to go a long way in the direction indicated. For
"America" here means, among other things, "the new world",
that is, in the present instance, another and that other world, in
comparison with the former world and this one. One cannot be
late for it (cf. "perhaps there is still time"), so that if a person
were delayed in this world, it would not follow that he had
arrived late there. In crossing the threshold of death a person
crosses the threshold of eternity. He falls asleep in a dream which,
like every dream, knows no ordinary count of time: "Once it
would seem to him that he had lain there for a month; another
time, that it was still the same day as he fell ill" [111]. Cf. also
[420] and later:

"Oh, you're not asleep. Well, here I am! [. . .]..."

"What time is it?" asked Raskolnikov, looking round in alarm.

"You've had a capital sleep, my dear chap; it's evening, it must be six o'clock [. . .]"

"Heavens! How could I? . . ."

"What is all this about? It's good for you. What is your hurry? Have you got an appointment, or something? We have all time before us". [122]

And later Porfiry's words to Raskolnikov: " 'Yes, yes, yes! Don't worry! There's plenty of time, plenty of time' " [320]; and also: " 'Good Lord! What are you talking about? [. . .] Please don't upset yourself [. . .] Plenty of time, plenty of time' " [322]. "Plenty of time" when there is none, when it has stopped.

The dreams tormenting Raskolnikov in his sleep of death and connected with "The Soul's Journey through Ordeals"[26] are presented in the logic indicated by the general situation: the hero is both alive and dead, he is both in this and the other world. But the "Soul's journey through ordeals" in *Crime and Punishment* is the subject of a special article.

Notes

1. The figures in square brackets are page references to Fyodor Dostoevsky, *Crime and Punishment,* translated by Jesse Coulson, with an introduction and notes by Richard Peace, Oxford World's Classics, Oxford, New York, 1981, 1995.

2. Vetlovskaya is here playing with the verbs *zapirat'* ("to lock"), its reflexive *zapirat'sya* ("to refuse to admit") and *otperet'sya* ("to open").

3. I.e. *proshlyapil*—a pun on the word for "hat", *shlyapa.*

4. Cf. the consonance of sound in *chert*—"devil" and—*chertochka*— "trait".

5. "*Shut te der-i-i!*" *Shut*—"clown" is a euphemism for the devil (cf. "joker"). Coulson has "Blast your eyes."

6. Vetlovskaya explains this as Dostoevsky playing with the Russian idiom: "was called Mitka" (*Mit'koy zvali*) indicating that someone has disappeared.

7. I. F. Annensky writes: "The devil has only entered the novel episodically, but, apparently, he holds a central, and in any case, significant place. That is beyond doubt". (Annensky, I. F. "Vtoraya kniga otrazheniy", Annensky, I, *knigi otrazheniy*, Moscow, 1979, p. 198). The author does not specify which episode, or episodes, he has in mind, but he correctly notes the general tendency.

8. The actual Russian is *iskupalsya*, which is highly ambiguous. It means "have you been bathing?" ("been to the bathhouse?"), but *iskupat'sya* also means "to redeem oneself".

9. *Prepodobnogo ottsa nashego Ioanna, igumena Sinayskoi gory*, "*Lestvitsa*", *v russkom perevode*, 7th edition, Sergiev Posad, 1908, p. 129.

10. *Sv. ottsa nashego Feodora Studita "Podvizhnicheskie monakham nastavleniya" // "Dobrotolubie"*, Sviato-Troitskaya Lavra, 1992, vol.4, pp. 409, 414 (cf. pp. 512–513).

11. *Otechnik, sostavlennyy svyatitelem Ignatiem (Bryanchaninovym)*, 3rd ed., St Petersburg, 1891, Part 1, p. 369. These four levels embrace the more subdivided categories of the sinful condition as a growing force, usually encountered in Orthodox asceticism. Cf. for example: *Prepodobnogo ottsa nashego Ioanna, igumena Sinayskoi gory, "Lestvitsa"*, p. 125. In all cases the sinful thought precedes the act. Cf. "Do not abuse thought, in order, that you will not then necessarily abuse things; for if you do not sin in thought beforehand, you will never sin in deed" (*Sv. Maksim Ispovednik // "Dobrotolyubie"*, vol.3, p. 191). The idea that the theory of Raskolnikov, which led him to the evil act, was his chief crime was expressed by one of the early critics of the novel—A.M. Bukharev. See on this: A.P. Dmitriev, "A.M. Bukharev (Arkhimandrit Feodor) kak literaturnyy kritik", *Khristianstvo i russkaya literatura*, St P., 1996, p. 191.

12. This is a transformation of a folklore motif: wealth acquired with the aid of unholy powers turns into junk, manure, disintegrates into dust, disappears (cf. for example, in Gogol's "The Bewitched Place"). In essence it is the same in Christian understanding, with the difference that here all wealth (of a material nature) is dust and ashes, and is not worth its bother.

13. *na arshine prostranstva*—Vetlovskaya is playing with the ambiguity of a recurrent phrase in the novel, translated by Coulson as a "hand's breadth of ground" [152, 164, (182 omitted by Coulson), 409].

14. *Izhe vo svyatykh ottsa nashego Ioanna Zlatoustogo, arkhiepiskopa Konstantinopol'skogo Izbrannye tvoreniya. "Besedy ot Ioanna Bogoslova"*, Moscow, 1993, vol.1, p. 55.

15. I.F. Annensky writes: "... punishment in the novel almost precedes the crime" (I. Annensky, "Vtoraya kniga otrazheniy", p. 191). If one links the idea of punishment with the hero's illness (and that is what one must do here) then the punishment actually begins before the crime (the fact of murder)—namely from the sinful thought that it is permissible. Before I.F. Annensky, and more precisely than he, a similar idea had been expressed by A.M. Bukharev, in whose opinion, Raskolnikov's evil deed itself, as the direct result of a criminal theory, was, in a certain sense "punishment" for it. See: A.P. Dmitriev, *A.M. Bukharev (arkhimandrit Feodor) kak literaturnyy kritik*, p. 192. A similar idea, from a different point, was reached by Sinya Kori in his paper "Smert' v syuzhetnom postroenii romana *Idiot*" ["Death in the plot structure of the novel *The Idiot*"] delivered in Staraya Russa in May 1996. See: *Dostoevsky: materialy i issledovaniya*, No.14, St Petersburg 1997, pp. 130–138. ("One can say that for Raskolnikov murder is a capital execution, crime is a punishment") *ibid.* p. 136. Cf. also V. Kozhinov: *"Prestuplenie i nakazanie"*, *Tri shedevra russkoy klassiki*, Moscow, 1971, pp. 175–76.

16. Kenosuke Nakamura has called particular attention to the fact that the chief hero of *Crime and Punishment* belongs to a "life of the dead" [*mertvaya zhizn'*]. He explains this observation in the context of characteristics peculiar to Dostoevsky's own psychology and his outlook on life (as it is understood by the researcher). See: K. Nakamura, "Dve kontseptsii zhizni v romane *Prestuplenie i nakazanie* (oshchushchenie zhizni i smerti v tvorchestve Dostoevskogo), *Dostoevsky i mirovaya kul'tura*: Al'manakh, No.1, pt.1, St Petersburg, 1993, pp. 89–120.

17. See "Zhitie prepodobnogo Maksima Ispovednika", *Zhitiya svyatykh, na russkom yazyke izlozhennye po rukovodstvu Chet'ikh-Miney sv. Dmitriya Rostovskogo*, Moscow, 1904, Bk. 5 (January), pt. 2, p. 215.

18. *Dostopamyatnye skazaniya o podvizhnichestve svyatykh i blazhennykh ottsov*, Svyato-Troitskaya Sergieva Lavra, 1993, p 111.

19. Cf. the gospel account of the curing of a man possessed: "Jesus [...] rebuked the foul spirit, saying unto him, *Thou* dumb and deaf spirit, I charge thee, come out of him, and enter no more into him" (Mark, 9, 25). Cf. also the motif of the grinding and gnashing of teeth: it is either devils, or sinners in their power, who grind and gnash their teeth.

20. Cf. Ephraim the Syrian [Efrem Sirianin], "Uroki o pokayanii", *Dobrotolyubie*, Vol. 2, p. 348.

21. See: *PSS*, Vol.6, pp. 5, 25, 35, 45, 93,111.

22. I.e. "rests", *pokoyitsia,* a word related to *pokoynyi,* "dead".

23. I.e. *kurolesit'.* Cf. *PSS.* 6, 194, 373.

24. Cf.: " 'But now I see that I don't want anything [. . .] anything at all. . . . I want nobody's help or pity . . . I myself . . . alone . . . Oh, that's enough! Leave me in peace!' " [106] and later about the old woman: " 'May she rest in peace and—enough, old woman, your time has come!' " [182] (*Tsarstvo ey nebesnoe i—dovol'no, matushka, pora na pokoy*).

25. For references to Svidrigaylov's "voyages" see: *PSS.* Vol. 6, pp. 222, 224, 237, 384–386, 394. Vetlovskaya is playing with the linguistic concept of *tot svet* in its sense of "the other world" and its later cold-war sense of "America" and the West in general.

26. *Khozhdenie dushi po mytarstvam.* The reference is to the chapter heading of chapter 3, Part 3 of Dostoevsky's novel *The Brothers Karamazov.* See *PSS,* Vol. 14, p. 412 and the explanation of the motif in *PSS,* Vol. 15, p. 579.

The Epilogue of *Crime and Punishment*

◆　◆　◆

> With striking clarity Dostoevsky sees the very
> moment of Christ's meeting with man, the
> sanctification of the earth and everything on it,
> sees it sensually and spiritually.
> —N. ABRAMOVICH, *Dostoevsky's Christ*

SOME TIME AGO, concerning the chief idea of *Crime and Punishment,* I wrote: "Only by the *one*, only through the *one*, can the other be saved. There is no other way."[1] The one embodies salvation for the other through the possibility of union with him—a possibility too infrequent and far from obvious, at all events, for that "other" in question—Raskolnikov. But for Dostoevsky there is only one salvation, which opens anew to the soul paths of union with the Living God. And Sonya not only embodies salvation, but presents an image visually perceived by Raskolnikov—an icon.

The preparation for the perception of the icon by Raskolnikov and the reader begins gradually, but openly and obviously—from the moment when the convicts' view of Sonya is described. Their attitude to her Raskolnikov finds incomprehensible and dismaying:

There was a question which he could not answer: why was Sonya so well liked by everybody? She did not try to ingratiate herself with them; they rarely met her, except occasionally at work, when she came to see him for a minute all knew her. Nevertheless, they knew besides that she had followed *him,* and knew how and where she lived. She did not give them money or perform any particular services for them. Once only, at Christmas, she brought a gift of pies and loaves for the whole prison. But little by little closer connexions developed between Sonya and them: she wrote letters for them to their families and posted them. When their relatives came to the town, the convicts told them to leave goods and even money for them in Sonya's care. Their wives and sweethearts knew her and visited her. And when she appeared [*yavlyalas'*—i.e. "manifested herself"—ED.], where they were working, to visit Raskolnikov, or when she met a party of prisoners on their way to work, they would all take off their caps and bow to her. 'Matushka, Sofya Semënovna, you are our kind, affectionate mother,' these coarse, branded criminals would say to the slight little creature. She would smile and bow to them; they were all pleased when she smiled at them. They liked even the way she walked, turning round to watch her, and praising her; they praised her even for being so small; they could not find enough to say in her praise. They even went to her to be cured. [523][2]

Reading this extract, one cannot help noticing that the convicts perceive Sonya as the image of the Madonna, which is particularly clear in the second part of the extract. What is described in the first part, if read without due attention, might be understood as the establishing of a relationship between the convicts and Sonya. But it is obvious that this is not quite so, for on one side a relationship is being established *before there are any relationships*: the convicts at once "so came to like Sonya". They *perceived* her immediately—and the dynamic of the description merely bears evidence to the fact that Sonya was becoming a protector and helper, consoler and intercessor for all the prison, which accepted her in this capacity even before any outward manifestations of the fact.

The second part (even as regards the lexical nuances of the author's language) points to the fact that something entirely special is taking place. This part begins with the amazing phrase: "and when she appeared [i.e. 'manifested herself']". The convicts' greeting is entirely consonant with "manifestation". "They all doffed their hats, they all bowed . . ." They call her "*matushka*" and "mother"; they love it when she smiles at them—a form of blessing. And, to crown everything, the manifested image of the Madonna proves to be miracle-working: "They even went to her to be cured".

It is highly characteristic that the convicts' attitude to Sonya is completely incomprehensible to Raskolnikov. He—an unbeliever—does not see what has been manifested to all around him. In order to emphasize that it is precisely this which is at issue: belief and unbelief, determining seeing and not seeing, the passage we have quoted is preceded by another, which tells of the attitude of the convicts to Raskolnikov and of the causes of this attitude:

> In the second week of Lent it was his turn, with the rest of his barrack, to prepare for the sacrament. He went to church and prayed with the others. Out of this, he himself did not know why, a quarrel arose one day; they all turned on him in fury:
> "You're an atheist! You don't believe in God!" they shouted. "We must kill you."
> He had never spoken to them about God or religious beliefs, but they wanted to kill him as an atheist; he did not reply to them, but was silent. . . . [522]

The way that these two passages we have quoted, follow on directly one from the other points to the fact that the convicts' dislike of Raskolnikov, their reverential love for Sonya (both without visible causes) and Raskolnikov's inability to understand their love are all merely different sides of the same question—that is, the question of faith. Raskolnikov does not *see*, but after enduring the impressions of hatred surrounding him, and the visions he has in his illness—he is prepared to see.

His readiness to see, the moment of anxious expectancy, are fixed by Dostoevsky in phrases full of ambiguities in a passage which comes immediately before the episode of the "manifestation":

> The second week of Easter was passing. . . . One evening Raskolnikov, who had almost completely recovered, had fallen asleep; when he woke up, he went by chance to the window and caught sight of Sonya in the distance, standing by the gates of the hospital; she *seemed to be waiting for something. It was as if something pierced his heart* at that moment; he shuddered, and moved hastily away from the window. [524–25 (emphasis added)]

Immediately after this Sonya falls ill and takes to her bed. She was waiting at the gates (at the gates of the soul) to come in.[3] It was now his turn to wait, worried and anxious.

> He was very disturbed and sent to inquire after her; he soon heard that her illness was not dangerous. When she in her turn heard that he was anxious and worried about her, Sonya sent him a note, written in pencil, informing him that she was much better, that she had simply had a slight cold, and that she would soon, very soon, come to see him at his work. As he read the note, his heart beat heavily and painfully. [525]

In his illness Raskolnikov sees nightmarish visions of the ways in which the ideal society might be ordered. As he gets better, it is the waiting Sonya he sees, and once he has recovered it is an icon: the image of the Madonna, and he bows down to it.

The moment of the icon's creation[4] is as though marked out, separated from the preceding text by the description of a state of special illumination for the hero, the removal of the action from the habitual flow of time, and its transference on to the plane of eternity, to penetrate into which icons must serve us as little windows:

There, in the immensity of the steppe, flooded with sun-light, the black tents of the nomads were barely visible dots. Freedom was there, there other people lived, so utterly un-like those on this side of the river that it seemed as though with them time had stood still, and the age of Abraham and his flocks was still the present. Raskolnikov sat on and his unwavering gaze remained fixed on the farther bank; his mind had wandered into day dreams; he thought of nothing, but an anguished longing disturbed and tormented him. [525]

From an analysis of "The Dream of the Comic Man"[5] we know that unconscious longing in the works of Dostoevsky appears as the pining of the part for the whole. And here, before us is the striving to unite with God, the rejected Father, in order to return to Abraham's bosom. And to the genuine call, which at last rings out, there is an immediate response. The two paragraphs of text which follow are the creation of the icon; the third paragraph is the veneration of the icon.

Suddenly Sonya appeared at his side. She had come up al-most soundlessly and sat down beside him. It was early; the chill of the morning still lingered. She wore her shabby old burnous and the green shawl. Her face still bore traces of her illness; it was thinner and paler and hollow-cheeked. She gave him a joyful welcoming smile, but she held out her hand as timidly as ever. [525]

Let us turn our attention first of all to Sonya's dress. She was wearing a *burnous* [Russian—*burnus*; Coulson has "pelisse"—ED.]. A *burnous* is a cloak and outer garment of various types, male and female, ostensibly based on an Arab model (Vl. Dal', *Tolkovyy slo-var'*). It is the *burnous*, a widely disseminated form of clothing, which most resembles the traditional clothing of Mary—the *Ma-foriy* (the dress of married Palestinian women). And then there is the green shawl or kerchief [*platok*]. Green in general, as the colour of life on earth, is directly linked to the image of the Madonna, who prays for and represents man, the earth and all earthly creatures before the Lord. It is constantly present even in icons. So, for example, the Madonna Hodegetria[6] from the Cathedral of the Nativity of the Virgin of the Ferapont Monastery (now in the Russian Museum in St Peterburg) is depicted with a green underside to her hood. The famous icon, originating in the workshop of Dionisiy, "All nature rejoices in Thee" [*O Tebe raduetsya*] from the Cathedral of the Dormition in the town of Dmitrov (now in the Tretyakovskiy Gallery in Moscow) depicts the Madonna in Glory sitting on a throne, surrounded by circles of dark blue and green light which emanate from the throne. If one recalls Sonya's almost colourless, soft, downy hair—it could fully present a halo, and the green shawl depict "Glory".[7]

There is, however, a more convincing interpretation of the green shawl within the structure of the novel itself. In terms of colour it is obviously to be compared with the cupola of the church which Raskolnikov sees in his dream of the little mare, and where there lives his God, whom he has lost and found anew: "In the cemetery was a stone church with a green cupola, where he came once or twice a year with his father and mother to a requiem in memory of his dead grandmother . . ." [52]. The cupola is the church's crown. In the icon "Intercessor for Sinners" the Madonna is traditionally depicted in a crown. In approaching Sonya, the hero once more comes close to the church of his childhood.

Sonya's face is pale, thin, sunken (as a result of which the eyes always assume greater size and seem to stand out from the face). This, I think, can be understood without commentary. But if one takes the expression of the face: there is greeting and joy in combination with a timidly held out hand (add timidity to the expression). This remarkably exactly conveys the impression, though fairly difficult to describe, which is left on one by icons depicting this type of gesture—one of prayer, caressing, greeting.

A circumstance must be noted, which from any other point of view would be strange, but is necessary for the manifestation of the visible icon on the pages of the novel—Sonya approaches silently and *sits down* beside Raskolnikov, after which she then stretches out her arm to him in greeting, without hailing him or greeting him verbally, as might be expected, and standing up immediately after appearing. But it is precisely such a pose which is necessary for the appearance of the Madonna alongside the "child", and here the possibility is that Raskolnikov himself might become the Christ child. A *possibility* to whose summons one might respond, but also might not, is here displayed more openly than in many other passages in the novel:[8]

> She always stretched out her hand to him timidly, some-times even half withdrawing it, as if she feared he would repulse her. He always grasped it reluctantly, always greeted her with a kind of irritation, sometimes remained obsti-nately silent all through her visit. There had been occasions when she had quailed before him and gone away deeply hurt. But this time their hands remained joined; he gave her a rapid glance, but said nothing and turned his eyes to the ground. They were alone; there was nobody to see them. The guard had turned away. [526]

Raskolnikov's gesture of taking Sonya's hand and holding it determines the nature of the icon. I am aware of only two types of icon in which Christ holds the hand of the Madonna: the Kiev-Bratskaya icon of the Madonna and the icon of the Madonna called "The Intercessor for Sinners" [*Sporuchnitsa greshnykh*]. In the Kiev-Bratskaya icon Christ holds the hand of the Madonna in one hand, the other is raised with fingers formed for a blessing. His gaze is directed upwards, His cheek is pressed to that of the Ma-donna. In the icon, *Sporuchnitsa greshnykh*, both of Christ's hands touch the hands of the Madonna. His gaze is directed ahead (com-pared with that of the Madonna, which is directed more down-wards). The figures leave one with the impression that they are, in fact, sitting side by side. In my view it is rather the second type of icon which appears in the novel's finale, but there is it seems a "thematic resonance" with the history of the Kiev-Bratskaya Madonna. I give it here in the words of the Orthodox Church Calendar for 1979:

The Kiev-Bratskaya icon of the most holy Madonna appeared in 1654 and was later to be found in Kiev, in a monastery (*Bratstkiy uchilishchnyy monastyr'*), though earlier it had been locally venerated in Vyshgorod. In 1862 the Crimean Tartars crossed the Dnepr near Vyshgorod, they seized it from the shrine along with sacred objects and other holy icons, but the miracle-working icon of the Madonna was cast into the Dnepr. It floated down the river to Kiev-Podol and came to a stop in the Dnepr opposite the Bratskiy monastery. Here it was joyfully accepted by the Orthodox monks and with all due honour transferred to their monastery. The feasts of the Kiev-Bratskiy icon of the Madonna are celebrated on 10th May, 2nd June and 6th September. (p. 58)

The arrival of the icon by river corresponds to the fact that in *Crime and Punishment* it is on the bank of a river that the icon is "created". Moreover, the place where it happens is particularly stressed and marked out, and also the "acceptance" of the icon by the Orthodox monks reminds me very much of Sonya's acceptance by the convicts.

Yet, all the same, the true heroine of the Epilogue of *Crime and Punishment* is "Sporuchnitsa greshnykh". This is what the *Complete Orthodox Theological Encyclopaedic Dictionary*[9] has to say about the icon:

> *Sporuchnitsa greshnykh* is an icon of the Madonna so called because in it the Madonna is depicted with the Christ child, holding Her right hand in both of His, as is done on completion of a contract. By this pressing of His Mother's hand, it is as though he is assuring Her that He will always listen to Her prayers for sinners. The icon's provenance and when it was painted is unknown, but it has been a wonder-working icon since 1844. It is celebrated on the 7th March and the 29th May.

And this is what the Orthodox Church Calendar (1979, p. 59) says of it:

> The icon of the Madonna *Sporuchnitsa greshnykh* was at one time in the Ordinskiy Monastery in the Orlov diocese,

where, in the 40s of the nineteenth century, it was famous
for its miracles. A copy of this miracle-working icon, placed
in the church of St Nikolai in Khamovniki in Moscow, became famous in 1848 for the light seen to come from it at
night, the exuding of holy oil and many other miracles. Of
all the miraculous healings by the icon of the Madonna
Sporuchnitsa greshnykh, there are more than 115 which have
been declared and recorded during its first six years. The
title of the icon of the Madonna "Intercessor for Sinners"
expresses the many and varied aspects of Her gracious love
for the sinful tribe of mankind, which she has shown
throughout all times.

There is a further addition to the description; several icons of
this type have an inscription, as though encircling the icon: "I
am the Intercessor for sinners to My Son / He has given me His
hand to listen to me always on their behalf / They always beg
me to grant them joy / Through me they get joy eternal".

The very fact that Sonya is accepted by the convicts as their
protectrice/intercessor [*zastupnitsa*] leads one to suppose that, for
the icon made manifest through her, no better title could be
thought of than *Sporuchnitsa greshnykh*. But the miracle itself, brought
about through her love for Raskolnikov, is also a miracle in salvation for a sinner, who has turned away from God (i.e. the most
devoid of hope in some sense). It also seems significant to me
that at the time of writing *Crime and Punishment* the icon *Sporuchnitsa
greshnykh* was a new wonder-working icon, quite recently, in "a
century of unbelief and doubt", reminding people of the endless
mercy of God and the Madonna's power of intercession.

But what is also interesting; immediately after the "creation"
of the icon, as has already been said, there follows Raskolnikov's
veneration of it:

How it happened he himself did not know, but suddenly
he seemed to be seized and cast at her feet. He clasped her
knees and wept. For a moment she was terribly frightened,
and her face grew white. She sprang up and looked down
at him, trembling. But at once, in that instant, she under-

stood. Infinite happiness shone in her eyes; she had understood, and she no longer doubted that he loved her, loved
her forever, and that now at last the moment had come.
. . . [526]

And further on, the whole of the last page of the novel is as
though permeated with a feeling of happiness, of life, of joy,
which changes everything, even the convicts' attitude to Raskolnikov, and the joy which has been granted them is eternal: "and
the heart of each held endless springs of life for the heart of the
other" [526]. The Madonna fulfills her promise: "Through me
they get joy eternal".

One could end here, but there is another icon which makes
us look at the whole reading of the text from a slightly different
angle. It is an icon of the *Hodegetria* type, in which (and it seems
untypical for this type of icon) Christ is also depicted holding the
hand of the Madonna. The poses of the figures in the icon
scarcely recall what is delineated in the text of the novel. The
Madonna leans towards Christ, but He, bent towards Her, has
turned his head and looks back over his left shoulder. This icon
of the Madonna is called "Of the Passion" [*Strastnaya*]. This is what
the *Orthodox Church Calendar* says about it:

> It received the title "Of the Passion" because on either side
> of the face of the most holy Mother of God it depicts two
> angels with the instruments of Christ's suffering. This holy
> icon first displayed its miracle of grace in Nizhniy Novgorod,
> curing the infirm peasant woman Evdokiya; after this the
> *Hodegetria* icon was taken to the village of Palitsi. In 1641 it
> was transferred to Moscow and at the place where it could
> be encountered, near the Tver Gate a convent was built in
> 1654, called "Of the Passion" [*Strastnyy*] after the icon. Cele-
> bration of this holy icon takes place on 13th August and
> on the sixth Sunday after Easter. [1979, p. 61]

What claims attention in this text is the information about the
celebration on the sixth Sunday after Easter. We are dealing here

with a "movable" feast, whose date is counted in the same fashion
as that in the Epilogue of *Crime and Punishment*. And, apparently,
this feast coincides with the "manifestation" of the icon in *Crime
and Punishment*. All this makes one look more closely at the dates
designated in similar fashion in the text, assuming that they have
not been fixed by chance.

The first date relates to a passage already cited, the first to
relate the "creation" of the icon—the scene in the church: "In
the second week of Lent it was his turn, with the rest of his
barrack, to prepare for the sacrament" [522]. The second week of
Lent is particularly devoted to *sin*. The reading on the Monday
includes the narrative of man's first and second sins—of the Fall,
and of Cain's envy of Abel, whose sacrifice was accepted by God.
The words of *Proverbs* 4, 10–22 sound as though directly addressed
to Raskolnikov:

> Hear, Oh my son, and receive my sayings; and the years of
> thy life shall be many/I have taught thee in the way of
> wisdom; I have led thee in right paths./When thou goest
> thy steps shall not be straitened; and when thou runnest
> thou shalt not stumble./Take fast hold of instruction; let *her*
> not go; keep her; for she *is* thy life./Enter not into the path
> of the wicked, and go not in the way of evil *men*./Avoid it,
> pass not by it, turn from it, and pass away./For they sleep
> not; except they have done mischief; and their sleep is taken
> away, unless they cause *some* to fall./For they eat the bread
> of wickedness, and drink the wine of violence./But the path
> of the just *is* as the shining light, that shineth more and
> more unto the perfect day./The way of the wicked *is* as
> darkness: they know not at what they stumble./My son,
> attend to my words; incline thine ear unto my sayings./Let
> them not depart from thine eyes; keep them in the midst
> of thine heart./For they *are* life unto those that find them,
> and health to all their flesh.

It is as though here there is an answer given to all his "objectless
and undirected anxiety in the present" [520] ["*trevogu bespredmetnuyu
i bestsel'nuyu*"] of the previous pages. There is a direct indication

here as to how he can again find his lost life. In reality, it is given to Raskolnikov to listen before seeing.

Regrettably space will not allow me to quote here all the Gospel readings for this week and the variants of the sermons, but, surprisingly, they are "included" in the text of *Crime and Punishment* as though quoted there. Frequently they take the form of particular "keys" which express in a direct way what Dostoevsky is "narrating". Here, for example, is the disquisition of Tikhon Zadonskiy on the words of the First Epistle of St John:

> Sin is illegality. What is sin? It is withdrawal from living and life-creating God. It is treachery, destruction of the oath given to God at baptism. It is the destruction of God's holy, just, eternal law, resistance to the holy and blessed will of the blessed God. It is to insult God's eternal and endless truth. It is to insult the great, infinite, ineffable, terrible, holy blessed and eternal God, the Father and the Son and the Holy Ghost, revered by the blessed spirits, the holy Angels.

And then this is what the prelate Grigoriy Nisskiy says about sin: "Sin is not an integral part of our nature, but a deviation from it. Just as illness and deformity are not inherent in our nature, but unnatural, so activity directed towards evil must be acknowledged as the distortion of our innate goodness."

Words, too, have done their work, but they are still dead in his soul until the revelation, until seeing, until the meeting with God. Therefore he keeps silent and utters no objections to the convicts, who want to kill him as an atheist. But he has heard that his sin is an illness, a deviation from life and health—and the illness which follows, a physical one, seems to signify a crisis. The illness has come out: "Raskolnikov was in hospital all through the latter part of Lent and Easter" [523].

The following event, marked by a date, is like a moment in which his heart opens, described in the vaguest of terms: "It was as if something pierced his heart at that moment" [525]. It is particularly interesting for the compression of time within it (let us not forget that the episode which follows unfolds as though in eternity). The "date" is described by Dostoevsky in the following manner: "The second week [*nedelya*] after Easter was passing. . . ." [524]. If the word *nedelya* is given its ecclesiastical sense, denoting a particular day of the week—Sunday, then the second *nedelya* (Sunday) after Easter (The Holy Resurrection of Christ)[10] is the Sunday of Thomas the Apostle. But the second Sunday after Holy Week is the Sunday of the women bearing spices. It is thus that the moment is designated of the meeting, taking place at last, of Sonya and Raskolnikov—of one who can only believe "having put in his fingers" and of the other who lovingly believed the word. This is what is read in Church for the week about Thomas (John, 20, 19–31):

> Then the same day at evening, being the first *day* of the week, when the doors were shut where the disciples were assembled for fear of the Jews, came Jesus and stood in the midst, and saith unto them, Peace *be* unto you./And when He had so said, He shewed unto them *His* hands and His side. Then were the disciples glad, when they saw the Lord./ Then said Jesus to them again, Peace *be* unto you; as *My* father hath sent Me, even so send I you./And when He had said this, He breathed on *them*, and saith unto them, Receive ye the Holy Ghost/Whose soever sins ye remit, they are remitted unto them; *and* whose soever *sins* ye retain, they are retained./But Thomas, one of the twelve called Didymus, was not with them when Jesus came./The other disciples therefore said unto him, We have seen the Lord. But he said unto them, Except I shall see in his hands the print of the nails, and put my finger into the print of the nails, and thrust my hand into his side, I will not believe./And after eight days again his disciples were within, and Thomas with them: *then* came Jesus, the doors being shut, and stood in the midst, and said, Peace *be* unto you./Then saith he to Thomas, Reach hither thy finger, and behold My hands; and reach hither thy hand, and thrust *it* into My side: and be not faithless but believing./And Thomas answered and said unto him, My Lord and my God./Jesus saith unto him,

Thomas, because thou hast seen Me, thou hast believed: blessed *are* they that have not seen, and *yet* have believed./ And many other signs truly did Jesus in the presence of his disciples, which are not written in this book:/ But these are written that ye might believe that Jesus is the Christ, the Son of God; and that believing ye might have life through His name.

John calls on us to believe in his words. If one recalls that it is precisely John's Gospel that Sonya reads to Raskolnikov on his first visit, then the words of the Sunday [Resurrection] Reading seem still more significant. This is what is said about the women bearing spices in the *Book of the Clergyman* (quoted from the Orthodox Calendar for 1993):

Many words and assurances were needed by Our Lord Jesus Christ in order to convince the Apostles of His Resurrection. But one word from an angel was sufficient for the women bearing spices to believe in the joyful news. Love and faithfulness that is what distinguished the women bearing spices. [. . .] Joseph and Nicodemus were secret disciples of Christ, but when Jesus was crucified and He died on the cross, love overcame fear, and they showed greater faithfulness than Christ's closest disciples. Convictions of the mind did not save the disciples from fear, but the love which filled Nicodemus and Joseph and the women bearing spices overcame everything.

But this is not all concealed behind the strange "date". This *nedelya* (in its lay sense of "week") ends with a Sunday on which there is a reading about the infirm. The illness of Raskolnikov and Sonya, before the miracle worked on them, resonates in a remarkable fashion with a passage in the Acts, which is read on that day, and commented on by adding the well-known story in John's gospel of Christ curing the man who had been waiting for a cure at the pool by the sheep market for thirty eight years. Meeting him later in the temple, Jesus sent him on his way cured:

"Behold, thou art made whole: sin no more, lest a worse thing come unto thee"(John, 5,14).

The Acts relate the curing of a righteous woman by Peter:

> Now there was at Joppa a certain disciple named Tabitha, which by interpretation is called Dorcas: this woman was full of good works and almsdeeds which she did./And it came to pass in those days that she was sick, and died: whom when they had washed, they had laid *her* in an upper chamber [. . .]Then Peter arose and went with them [the men sent to him by the disciples—*T.K.*]. When he was come they brought him into the upper chamber: and all the widows stood by him weeping, and shewing the coats and garments which Dorcas made, while she was with them.

I must point out here that Sonya, having followed Raskolnikov, "did sewing and, since there was no dressmaker in the town, had become indispensable in many houses" [519]. But let us continue the reading of the Acts: "But Peter put them all forth, and kneeled down, and prayed; and turning *him* to the body said, Tabitha arise. And she opened her eyes and when she saw Peter, she sat up./And he gave her *his* hand, and lifted her up, and when he had called the saints and widows, presented her alive" (Acts 9, 36–37, 39, 41). Here, it seems to me, mutuality is being stressed and what is general in the resurrection of the protagonists; for not only the ancient cripple and the sinner, but the righteous woman who is dying has need of *another* in order to be resurrected.

But in this way the date indicated subsumes the second, third, and fourth week after Easter. But in the sixth week (the sixth Sunday) after Easter, the feast of *Strastnaya* ["Of the Passion"] is celebrated. It is the celebration of yet another icon, as I have already said, where Christ is depicted holding the Madonna by the hand. Following the text of the Epilogue one might rightly suppose that about two weeks pass between the two meetings of the protagonists.

Therefore, of course, we are looking at a synthetic image, although I still think that the icon of the Madonna *Sporuchnitsa greshnykh* has the greatest significance for its composition. But the essential here lies not in any analytical search. The essential here is that Dostoevsky's text is permeated with multiple sense, which is, as it were, located in a "subtext", to which, however, any interested reader can have absolutely open access, but at the same time this sense can still be perceived emotionally, and in order to "feel a thought" (an expression much loved by Dostoevsky) it is sufficient to have the text of the novel and the images it gives of man's meeting with God, which "Dostoevsky sees with striking clarity, sees it sensually and spiritually."

Notes

1. See: T. Kasatkina, *Kharakterlogiya Dostoevskogo*, Moscow, 1996, pp. 93, 108.

2. The numbers in square brackets are page references to: Fyodor Dostoevsky, *Crime and Punishment*, translated by Jesse Coulson, with an introduction and notes by Richard Peace, OUP, Oxford, New York, 1998. Here the translation has been slightly amended to coincide with Kasatkina's text. Coulson translates *matushka* as "little mother", but Kasatkina points out that this, rather than a diminutive, is a term of endearment often applied to the Madonna herself.

3. Cf. *Revelations*, Ch.3, v. 20: "Here I stand knocking at the door: if anyone hears my voice and opens the door I will come in and sit down to supper with him and he with me."

4. Tatyana Kasatkina explains the phenomenon in the following terms: "What is meant is that the icon does not just occur on its own, but is created by the united efforts and will of the author and the characters at the moment when text and readers are prepared for such a creation."

5. *Son smeshnogo cheloveka*: a short story by Dostoevsky written in 1877. See: T. Kasatkina, *op. cit.*, pp. 33–53.

6. This type of icon, the Madonna Hodegetria, shows the Virgin Mary as a guide, She who leads along the path of salvation.

7. It was along these lines that I interpreted Sonya's green shawl, when I discussed the icon of the Epilogue of *Crime and Punishment* in Staraya Russa [at a conference held in May 1996 at the Dostoevsky museum there—ED.]. Moreover, I had already said then (why will be

explained later) that the icon manifested to Raskolnikov was a completely identifiable one "*Sporuchnitsa greshnykh*" [Intercessor for Sinners]. The following day, after my paper, we went to the Khutynskiy Monastery, where, after attending a requiem mass for Derzhavin [famous 18th-century poet buried there—ED.] we went to look round the monastery. There were a fairly large number of new style icons there. The majority of these (more than five) were icons of the "*Sporuchnitsa greshnykh*", which in itself is quite unusual, as it is not the most widespread type of icon. But what was entirely surprising, almost all depicted the Madonna in a bright green dress! Perhaps this was a willful interpretation of events on my part, but I took this as confirmation of my surmise.

8. But even there it is displayed fairly obviously, even challengingly: thus when Porfiry already has all the cards in his hands, the Lord defends Raskolnikov from a *forced* admission, by at that very moment "bringing up" Mikolka with his admission.

9. Polnyy pravoslavnyy bogoslovskiy entsiklopedicheskiy slovar' (St Petersburg, n.d.) reprinted Moscow, 1992, vol. 2, pp. 2110–11.

10. *Voskresenie* means "resurrection", but it is also the more usual word for "Sunday."

Suggested Reading

◆ ◆ ◆

Anderson, Roger B. *Dostoevsky: Myths of Duality.* Gainesville, FL: University of Florida Press, 1986.

————. "*Crime and Punishment*: Psycho-Myth and the Making of a Hero." *California Slavic Studies* 11(1977), 523–38.

Blackmur, R. P. "*Crime and Punishment*: Murder in Your Own Room." *Eleven Essays in the European Novel.* New York: Harcourt Brace & World, 1964, 119–140.

Bloom, Harold, ed. *Raskolnikov and Svidrigailov.* Philadelphia: Chelsea House, 2004.

Breger, Louis. *Dostoevsky: The Author as Psychoanalyst.* New York: New York University Press, 1989.

Brody, Ervin C. "Meaning and Symbolism in the Names of Dostoevsky's *Crime and Punishment* and *The Idiot.*" *Names* 27, 2 (June 1979), 117–40.

Burnett, Leon, ed. *F. M. Dostoevsky (1821–1881): A Centenary Collection.* Colchester, UK: University of Essex, 1981.

Busch, Robert, L. *Humor in the Major Novels of Dostoevsky.* Columbus, OH: Slavica, 1987.

Cassedy, Steven. "The Formal Problem of the Epilogue in *Crime and Punishment*: The Logic of Tragic and Christian Structures." *Dostoevsky Studies* 3 (1982), 171–90.

Catteau, Jacques. *Dostoyevsky and the Process of Literary Creation*. Trans. Audrey Littlewood. Cambridge: Cambridge University Press, 1989.

Conradi, Peter J. *Fyodor Dostoevsky*. New York: St. Martin's Press, 1988.

Dostoevsky, Anna. *Dostoevsky: Reminiscences*. Trans. and ed. B. Stillman. New York: Liveright, 1975.

Dostoevsky, Fyodor. *Crime and Punishment*, World's Classics ed. Trans. Jesse Coulson, with intro., bibliography, and notes by R. Peace. Oxford and New York: Oxford University Press, 1995.

Frank, Joseph. *Dostoevsky: The Seeds of Revolt 1821–1849*. Princeton: Princeton University Press, 1976.

———. *Dostoevsky: The Years of Ordeal 1850–1859*. Princeton: Princeton University Press, 1983.

———. *Dostoevsky: The Stir of Liberation 1860–1865*. Princeton: Princeton University Press, 1986.

———. *Dostoevsky: The Miraculous Years 1865–1871*. Princeton: Princeton University Press, 1995.

———. *Dostoevsky: The Mantle of the Prophet 1871–1881*. Princeton: Princeton University Press, 2002.

Freeborn, Richard. *Dostoevsky: Life and Times*. London: Haus Publishing, 2003.

Gibian, George. "Traditional Symbolism in *Crime and Punishment*." *PMLA* 70 (Dec. 1955), 979–96.

———, ed. *Feodor Dostoevsky: Crime and Punishment*. The Coulson Translation. Backgrounds and Sources. Essays in Criticism. New York: W. W. Norton, 1964.

Hingley, Ronald. *The Undiscovered Dostoyevsky*. London: Hamish Hamilton, 1962.

Ivanov, Vyacheslav. "The Revolt Against Mother Earth." *Freedom and the Tragic Life. A Study in Dostoevsky*. Trans. Norman Cameron, ed. S. Konovalov. New York: The Noonday Press, 1952, 70–85.

Jackson, Robert Louis. *The Art of Dostoevsky: Deliriums and Nocturnes*. Princeton: Princeton University Press, 1981.

———. *Dialogues with Dostoevsky: The Overwhelming Questions*. Stanford: Stanford University Press, 1993.

———. *Dostoevsky: New Perspectives*. Englewood Cliffs, NJ: Prentice-Hall, 1984.

Johnson, Leslie A. *The Experience of Time in* Crime and Punishment. Columbus, OH: Slavica, 1985.

Johnson, Tamara, ed. *Readings on Fyodor Dostoyevsky*. San Diego: Greenhaven Press, 1988.

Jones, Malcolm V. *Dostoevsky: The Novel of Discord.* New York: Barnes & Noble, 1976.

———Jones, Malcolm V., and Garth M. Terry, eds. *New Essays on Dostoevsky.* Cambridge: Cambridge University Press, 1983.

———. *Dostoevsky After Bakhtin: Readings in Dostoevsky's Fantastic Realism.* Cambridge: Cambridge University Press, 1990.

Jones, John. *Dostoevsky.* Oxford: Clarendon Press, 1983.

Kjetsaa, Geir. *Fyodor Dostoyevsky: A Writer's Life.* Trans. Siri Hustvedt and David McDuff. New York: Viking, 1987.

Kraeger, Linda, and Joe Barnhart. *Dostoevsky on Evil and Atonement.* Lewiston, NY: Edwin Mellen Press, 1992.

Krag, Erik. *Dostoevsky: The Literary Artist.* New York: Humanities Press, 1976.

Kravchenko, Maria. *Dostoevsky and the Psychologists.* Amsterdam: Verlag Adolf M. Hakkert, 1978.

Lanz, Kenneth. *The Dostoevsky Encyclopedia.* Westport, CT: Greenwood Press, 2004.

Leatherbarrow, William J. *Fedor Dostoevsky.* Boston: Twayne, 1981.

———. "Raskolnikov and the 'Enigma of His Personality'." *Forum for Modern Language Studies* 9 (1973): 153–65.

Lynch, Michael F. "Dostoevsky and Richard Wright: Choices of Individual Freedom and Dignity." *Chiba Review* 12 (1990), 25–40.

Martinsen, Deborah, A. "Shame and Punishment." *Dostoevsky Studies,* New Series, 5 (2001), 51–69.

Maze, J. R. "Dostoyevsky: Epilepsy, Mysticism, and Homosexuality." *American Imago* 38 (1981), 155–83.

Meijer, J. M. "Situation Rhyme in a Novel of Dostoevskij." *Dutch Contributions to the Fourth International Congress of Slavicists..* 'S-Gravenhage: Mouton & Co. (1958), 115–128.

Miller, Robin Feur, ed. *Critical Essays on Dostoevsky.* Boston: G.K. Hall, 1986.

Mochulsky, Konstantin. *Dostoevsky: His Life and Work.* Trans. Michael A. Minihan. Princeton: Princeton University Press, 1967.

Morson, Gary Saul. "How to Read *Crime and Punishment.*" *Commentary* 93, no.6 (June 1992), 49–53.

Nuttall, A. D. *Crime and Punishment: Murder as Philosophic Experiment.* Edinburgh: Published for Sussex University Press by Scottish Academic Press, 1978.

Peace, Richard. "Dostoyevsky and Tolstoy as Novelists of Ideas." *Transactions of Russian-American Scholars in the U.S.A.,* vol. 14. New York (1981), 231–38.

———. "Dostoevsky and the Concept of Many-Faceted Doubling." *XXI Vek glazami Dostoevskogo: Perspektivy chelovechestva* (Papers of International

Conference at University of Chiba, Japan, 2000), Moscow: Graal' (2002), 191–198.

Rahv, Philip. "Dostoevsky in *Crime and Punishment.*" *Partisan Review* 27 (Summer, 1960), 393–425.

Rice, James. "Raskol'nikov and Tsar Gorox." *Slavic and East European Journal* 25, no.3 (Fall 1981), 38–53.

———. *Dostoevsky and the Healing Art.* Ann Arbor: Ardis, 1985.

Rising, Catherine. "Raskolnikov and Razumov: From a Passive to Active Subjectivity in *Under Western Eyes.*" *Conradiana: A Journal of Joseph Conrad Studies* 33, no.1 (Spring 2001), 24–39.

Simmons, Ernest J. "In the Author's Laboratory," "Raskolnikov," and "The Art of *Crime and Punishment.*" *Dostoevsky: The Making of a Novelist.* London and New York: Oxford University Press, 1940, 139–183.

Straus, Nina Pelikan. *Dostoevsky and the Women Question.* New York: St. Martin's Press, 1994.

Terras, Victor. *FM. Dostoevsky: Life, Work, and Criticism.* Fredericton, Canada: York Press, 1984.

Villadsen, Preben. *The Underground Man and Raskolnikov* (trans. from Danish Daniel R. Frickelton and Laurits Rendboe). Odense: Odense University Press, 1981.

Wasiolek, Edward, ed. *Crime and Punishment and the Critics.* San Francisco: Wadsworth, 1961.

———, ed. and trans. *The Notebooks for Crime and Punishment.* Chicago and London: University of Chicago Press, 1967.

Wellek, René, ed. *Dostoevsky: A Collection of Critical Essays.* Englewood Cliffs, NJ: Prentice-Hall, 1964.

———. "Bakhtin's View of Dostoevsky: 'Polyphony' and 'Carnivalesque'," *Dostoevsky Studies*, 1 (1980), 31–39.

Index

◆ ◆ ◆